G000231144

'Academic research is making the case th
does have positive health benefits. In
clinicians to explain, from their direct c
think spiritual care is and why they believe it matters. This is a rare
opportunity that will inform practice and debate.'
— *The Revd Dr Steve Nolan, Princess Alice Hospice,*
Esher, and The University of Winchester

'This welcome and innovative book does not begin with a presumption
that there is a single definition of spirituality. It is, above all, a book of
stories, full of joy and pathos, which tell of what it means to be human. As
such, it deserves to be read by all those who wish to develop and enhance
their professional practice in informed, compassionate and integrated
ways.'
— *The Rev Dr Jonathan Pye, Honorary Research Fellow,*
Centre for Ethics in Medicine, University of Bristol

'The clarity, compassion and sheer humanity of the contributors make
this a great resource for students and professionals alike.'
— *The Revd Canon Dr Margaret Whipp, practical and*
pastoral theological educator, former consultant oncologist
and Lead Chaplain, Oxford University Hospitals

'Will re-energise anyone working in healthcare. Whether you are with
or without faith, this book will inspire those wanting to take seriously
spiritual life as a dimension of, and a resource for, recovery and wholeness.'
— *Kathryn Darby, Chaplain at Birmingham Children's Hospital and*
co-author of Spiritual Care with Sick Children and Young People

'The range of medical and psychological specialisms is diverse. It is an
exciting book with emphasis on listening to patients' stories and an active
concern for the wellbeing of patients.'
— *Marian Carter, author of* Helping Children and Adolescents
Think about Death, Dying and Bereavement

'Peter Wells has captured the importance of connecting body and soul
in spiritual care as an integral part of healthcare. Reading this book will
give other professionals the confidence to make similar connections.'
— *Alister Bull, author of* Assessing and Communicating
the Spiritual Needs of Children in Hospital

of related interest

Psycho-Spiritual Care in Health Care Practice
Edited by Guy Harrison
ISBN 978 1 78592 039 4
eISBN 978 1 78450 292 8

Chaplaincy in Hospice and Palliative Care
Edited by Karen Murphy and Bob Whorton
Foreword by Baroness Finlay of Llandaff
ISBN 978 1 78592 068 4
eISBN 978 1 78450 329 1

Assessing and Communicating the Spiritual Needs of Children in Hospital
A new guide for healthcare professionals and chaplains
Alister Bull
ISBN 978 1 84905 637 3
eISBN 978 1 78450 116 7

What Counsellors and Spiritual Directors Can Learn from Each Other
Ethical Practice, Training and Supervision
Edited by Peter Madsen Gubi
ISBN 978 1 78592 025 7
eISBN 978 1 78450 271 3

Spiritual Care in Common Terms
How Chaplains Can Effectively Describe the Spiritual
Needs of Patients in Medical Records
Gordon J. Hilsman, D.Min.
Foreword by James H. Gunn
ISBN 978 1 78592 724 9
eISBN 978 1 78450 369 7

Art of Living, Art of Dying
Spiritual Care for a Good Death
Carlo Leget
Foreword by George Fitchett
ISBN 978 1 78592 211 4
eISBN 978 1 78450 491 5

TREATING BODY AND SOUL

A Clinicians' Guide to Supporting
the Physical, Mental and
Spiritual Needs of Their Patients

Edited by
Peter Wells

Jessica Kingsley *Publishers*
London and Philadelphia

Contains public sector information licensed under the Open Government Licence v3.0

First published in 2017
by Jessica Kingsley Publishers
73 Collier Street
London N1 9BE, UK
and
400 Market Street, Suite 400
Philadelphia, PA 19106, USA

www.jkp.com

Library of Congress Cataloging in Publication Data
A CIP catalog record for this book is available from the Library of Congress

British Library Cataloguing in Publication Data
A CIP catalogue record for this book is available from the British Library

ISBN 978 1 78592 148 3
eISBN 978 1 78450 417 5

Printed and bound in Great Britain

*To the patients, relatives and staff with whom I have had
the privilege to journey in their spiritual need and care.*

Acknowledgments

The origins of writing this book came at the suggestion of one of the Senior Commissioning Editors of Jessica Kingsley Publishers, who attended a workshop I had facilitated and who subsequently invited me to put forward a proposal. I am grateful to have had the opportunity to collaborate with a wide variety of clinicians across several areas of medicine, inviting them to share their reflections as to why 'spiritual' care is so important, and to the varied ways the 'spiritual' can be thought of and explored with patients. So, to my editor and each author, my thanks.

My thanks must go to the many patients, relatives and staff with whom I have had the opportunity to explore my own understanding of spiritual need and spiritual care in the context of receiving healthcare. Their experience has certainly enriched mine, and the journey continues.

Special thanks go to two people who helped read each contribution in the preparation for delivering the manuscript to the publisher. The wisdom and guidance of Judy and Heather were invaluable.

And thanks to my partner, Nigel, who works in palliative care, and with whom I have shared many experiences of the patients we have each met. We are both constantly amazed, puzzled, delighted and sceptical at the breadth and depth of what being spiritual means when facing the end of life.

My thanks to everyone for their part in this book, and what it means to offer and provide spiritual care.

Contents

Introduction

WHY BOTHER? DOES IT REALLY MATTER?

Peter Wells

Peter Wells is Lead Chaplain at the Royal Sussex County Hospital. He was previously a hospice chaplain and Head of Allied Health Professionals. He has been involved in teaching how to support patients and their spiritual needs to medical students and nursing staff, as well as non-clinical staff who support patients. His experience has led him to believe that if the staff in healthcare can ask patients about what gives their life meaning and purpose, this brings the staff much richer information in caring for the patient, and lets the patient know that their needs are being taken seriously. Peter is an Anglican priest, honorary Canon of Chichester Cathedral and an accredited sex and relationship therapist and supervisor with COSRT.

The briefest of online searches will uncover a wide range of books and articles on patients requiring healthcare services and their religious needs, as well as the religious influences and rituals at various stages of healthcare, and the role of the chaplain in facilitating the religious needs of both patients and staff. As not everyone is religious, this book takes a much broader look, and aims to provide those who work in healthcare with a 'window' into trying to support the spiritual needs of patients, and how a wide variety of clinicians aim to support their patients in both body and soul.

Anyone who needs to use any of our healthcare services knows how busy they can be and how long it can take to be booked in for an appointment and then wait for further appointments. When the appointment comes, patients can be anxious that there will be so little time that they will not be able to discuss everything they want to because the clinicians will have many other people to see. There can surely only be time to talk about one or two issues and then out or on to the next clinic. In such a pressurised scenario why would you be able to talk about anything other than the body, and does anything else matter?

When young, I always remember older members of my family saying, 'you should never talk about sex, politics and religion; they are personal and private matters'. This led to the feeling that these must be very important issues to be kept secret. Alas, this means that there is no one you can talk to about such issues, and no one will want to talk to you about them either. You are on your own! Maybe I felt the call to be a cleric so that I would find out some of the answers and find others to talk to. As for the other two issues...?! Over the years social attitudes have changed, and the internet and social media now make every subject available, with a vast amount of information and debate, some very helpful, others very unhelpful.

Even in the 21st century there is, for some, a lingering notion that such issues as religion are still very personal and should not be discussed or mentioned. Add this notion to the reports of healthcare professionals seemingly imposing their personal beliefs on to their patients, and asking patients about anything other than physical symptoms is no easy task. Addressing the needs of the body and soul can be complex, and some healthcare professionals might consider that the needs of the body should be addressed by some healthcare professionals whilst the soul is attended to by other healthcare professionals. This division might be helpful to some, but how helpful is it to the patient, and to the healthcare clinician who regards patients as whole people? The division is really unhelpful and an anathema to providing holistic healthcare.

The years of being involved in healthcare have taught me that spirituality is much wider than religion, and that the body is more than the physical as it has a soul – all of which together are greater than the sum of their parts. Our journey through life is a composite one, made up of many elements interacting and reverberating with those around us, with the past, the present and our thoughts for the future. I know that spiritual care is not the preserve of the chaplain alone, and I know that clinicians trained to focus on the physical or mental have a great appreciation of their patients' stories and needs, their spirituality.

Both body and soul, both patient and clinician, need help in coming together to provide as much information and support as possible whilst someone requires healthcare services.

I wanted to give clinicians the chance to tell their story as to what they believe about body and soul. How do they engage with their patients in order to bring together their physical and spiritual needs? What I knew as I began to approach clinicians was that I was asking the converted! When I asked doctors, nurses and a radiographer to write about the way they work, most replied, 'I just do the job. I have never thought about how I do it.' My experience of them as clinicians, and their reputation, is that they, along with many others, are not just 'doing the job' of responding to physical symptoms but in many subtle, and sometimes not so subtle, ways, they are finding out the impacts on their patients' symptoms that can be regarded as spiritual and why it matters to find out. Due to a variety of expectations and interpretations, both within healthcare and without, the finding out is not easy.

Why bother with the 'spiritual' issues in healthcare when you have a chaplain?

My experience of meeting a broad cross-section of people in various healthcare settings is that when people need to access healthcare, whether needing an appointment with their general practitioner (GP), getting admitted to hospital following an acute episode or for an elective procedure, several things can happen:

- they are not in control of what is happening to them
- they hear and see a lot that they do not understand
- they can have a lot of time to think about life and what might happen
- they have a lot of time to mull over what is important in their lives, and what matters to them
- they write a story in their mind as to what is happening to them, their loved ones, their life

- questions and queries can begin to surface that they had not considered before.

As these can lead to questions and concerns as to what is important in life, and about existence and mortality, I regard these issues as being spiritual and not necessarily religious. There may or may not be a religious context, but this would be dependent on whether the individual had a religious affiliation or not. They are certainly issues that can have a profound impact on how people make decisions about their healthcare and how they view life, which is spirituality at its heart.

If a patient is experiencing these issues whilst they are seeing their healthcare clinician, this could provide valuable information in responding to the physical and/or mental symptoms that the patient presents with. The General Medical Council (GMC 2013) has already established the need to include these issues:

15. You must provide a good standard of practice and care. If you assess, diagnose or treat patients, you must:
   a) adequately assess the patient's conditions, taking account of their history (including the symptoms and psychological, spiritual, social and cultural factors), their views and values; where necessary, examine the patient
   b) promptly provide or arrange suitable advice, investigations or treatment where necessary
   c) refer a patient to another practitioner when this serves the patient's needs.

And in nursing care in 2010 the Royal College of Nursing produced *Spirituality in Nursing Care: A Pocket Guide*, in which it is stated:

The Nursing and Midwifery Council expects newly qualified graduate nurses to be able to: 'in partnership with the person, their carers and their families, make a holistic, person centred and systematic assessment of physical, emotional, psychological, social, cultural and spiritual needs, including risk, and together, develop a comprehensive personalised plan of nursing care.'

On the NHS England website, in the section entitled 'NHS Chaplaincy Programme', it is set out clearly why asking about spirituality and religion is necessary to patient care:

> The NHS Chaplaincy Programme is part of NHS England's drive to ensure good patient care and compliance with policy and legislation:
>
> - Compliance with the legal duties in the Equality Act 2010 – ensuring due regard to the protected characteristics on religion and belief.
> - Compliance with the NHS Constitution Principle 1 of ensuring comprehensive service for all irrespective of gender, race, disability, age, religion, belief.
> - Compliance with NHS England's business planning for 2013–14 'Putting people first' Priority 8 in promoting equality and reducing inequalities in health outcomes and the Five Year Forward View on Empowering Patients and Engaging Communities.
>
> (NHS England 2015a)

Chaplains have written a number of books about spiritual care. This book doesn't look at the role of the chaplain, but at how clinicians working in various disciplines of medicine define for themselves what is 'spiritual' and how relevant they consider it to be, and how they elicit from the patient information that can inform the clinician as to what is impacting on the patient's symptoms and how they can respond to the whole person. It can, however, be confusing to know what is meant by 'spirituality'.

Who defines what is spirituality?

However we might describe the process, some words keep on developing, evolving or changing, and 'spirituality' is one of those words. At times it seems that whomever you talk to has a different definition. In what follows are just a few examples of the current debate as to how some organisations and institutions define what they mean when they use the term 'spirituality'.

NHS ENGLAND

In 2015 NHS England produced revised guidance that was first published in 2003. In the document entitled *NHS Chaplaincy Guidelines 2015: Promoting Excellence in Pastoral, Spiritual and Religious Care*, the following is stated:

> *Spiritual care* is care provided in the context of illness which addresses the expressed spiritual, pastoral and religious needs of patients, staff and service users. These needs are likely to include one or more of the following:
>
> - ways to support recovery
> - issues concerning mortality
> - religious convictions, rituals and practices
> - non-religious convictions and practices
> - relationships of significance
> - a sense of the sacred
> - exploration of beliefs
>
> It is important to note that people who do not hold a particular religious affiliation may still require pastoral support in times of crisis.
>
> *Religion or belief* is as defined in the 2006 Equality Act: (a) 'religion' means any religion, (b) 'belief' means any religious or philosophical belief, (c) a reference to religion includes a reference to lack of religion, and (d) a reference to belief includes a reference to lack of belief. (NHS England 2015b)

ROYAL COLLEGE OF PSYCHIATRISTS

Psychiatry and spirituality have not always had an easy relationship, but in recent years the Royal College of Psychiatrists has had a Spirituality and Psychiatry Special Interest Group. On the College's website is the following:

What is spirituality?

There is no one definition, but in general, spirituality:

- is something everyone can experience
- helps us to find meaning and purpose in the things we value
- can bring hope and healing in times of suffering and loss
- encourages us to seek the best relationship with ourselves, with others and what lies beyond.

These experiences are part of being human – they are just as important to people with intellectual disability or other conditions, such as dementia and head injury, as they are in anybody else.

Spirituality often becomes more important in times of emotional stress, physical and mental illness, loss, bereavement and the approach of death.

All healthcare tries to relieve pain and to cure – but good healthcare tries to do more. Spirituality emphasises the healing of the person, not just the disease. It views life as a journey, where good and bad experiences can help you to learn, develop and mature. (RCPsych no date)

And to reflect that it is not only in healthcare that there are different interpretations, two non-healthcare examples follow.

ROYAL SOCIETY OF ARTS

In 2014 the Royal Society of Arts (RSA) produced a report entitled *Spiritualise: Revitalising Spirituality to Address 21st Century Challenges*. The report argues for 'reimagining' the spiritual in four ways, one of which is:

Spirituality is ambiguously inclusive by its nature and cannot be easily defined, but at heart it is about the fact that we are alive at all, rather than our personality or status it's about our 'ground' in the world rather than our 'place' in the world. It is possible and valuable to give spirituality improved intellectual grounding and greater cultural and political salience. The primary spiritual injunction is to know what you are as fully and deeply as possible. (RSA 2014, p.7)

Another way the RSA report aims to reimagine the spiritual is:

Spirituality struggles to differentiate itself from religion on the one hand, and wellbeing on the other... Our inquiry led us to four main features of human existence that help with this process, and unpack what it means to say the spiritual is about our 'ground' not our 'place':

- Love – the promise of belonging
- Death – the awareness of being
- Self – the path of becoming
- Soul – the sense of beyondness.

(RSA 2014, p.8)

In attempting to define spirituality, the RSA report quotes Sheldrake's definition:

Spirituality is a word that, in broad terms, stands for lifestyles and practices that embody a vision of human existence and of how the human spirit is to achieve its full potential. In that sense 'spirituality' embraces an aspiration approach, whether religious or secular, to the meaning and conduct of human life. (2012, p.17)

AN EXAMPLE IN THE UK NATIONAL PRESS
On the 500th anniversary of the Christian Reformation in Europe in 2016, *The Guardian* newspaper published this opinion:

The great question confronting Europe now is whether the values of liberal democracy can sustain themselves. Through the fat years when religion faded it seemed that an appeal to reason and self-interest was enough. In the age of Trump, of Brexit, and the Polish Law and Justice party it is obvious that it is not. Emotion and imagination are needed too, and these are the qualities that make up spirituality. Without a belief that human rights are a way of talking about objective reality, and that morality – however disputed – is a matter of fact and not of preference, the web of trust and decency that holds our societies together could be ripped to shreds.

The following example is from a chaplaincy perspective.

UNITED KINGDOM BOARD OF HEALTHCARE CHAPLAINCY

In 2009, the United Kingdom Board of Healthcare Chaplaincy (UKBHC) created a set of *Standards for Healthcare Chaplaincy Services*. In the document UKBHC use the following definitions:

Spiritual and religious care

- Religious care is given in the context of shared religious beliefs, values, liturgies and lifestyle of a faith community.
- Spiritual care is usually given in a one to one relationship, is completely person centred and makes no assumptions about personal conviction or life orientation.

(UKBHC 2009, p.4)

The UKBHC definitions have been adopted and adapted by various NHS Trusts. At Brighton and Sussex University Hospitals NHS Trust the following adapted version is used in the Trust's *Religion and Belief Policy*:

Spiritual care is completely person centred and makes no assumptions about personal conviction or life orientation and focuses on whatever belief animates or gives their life purpose which may or may not include a god.

Religious care supports patient choice regarding beliefs, rites and cultural traditions which are practised by specific groups. (2015, p.3)

My personal working interpretation endorses the above, but I am keen that there is a dynamic element to spirituality that is about movement and action.

Spirituality is whatever animates someone, giving their life meaning and purpose that transcends and permeates the essence of who they are and motivates their actions. This may or may not include a belief in a god or gods, but impacts on how they respond to life's events.

Religion is whatever binds a group of people together in their doctrine, dogma and beliefs to a god or gods. These doctrines, dogmas and beliefs should animate and thus combine the religious with the spiritual.

How people live out their understanding of spirituality and religions varies widely. My experience has been that for many people who have a religious affiliation, their faith forms and informs their spirituality and they would not differentiate one from the other. There are also people who have a religious affiliation and sit lightly towards some, or many, of the practices and dogmas, but who hold on to the tenets of the faith that their religion is based on. This leads to people claiming the same religious affiliation but living it out in a different way, which means that assumptions should not be made that all people who claim the same religious affiliation will live it out in the same way. There are also a large number of people who would not describe themselves as religious but who do believe in some form of 'divine' presence, and for whom such beliefs are very important but who find it difficult to articulate out of concern to not appear disrespectful or non-committal. There are also religious people who understand the doctrine and dogmas as to what binds them together but alas, the beliefs do not animate them or permeate their lives. People who regard themselves as spiritual and not at all religious will often comment, in a halting and guilty way, that they are not sure what they do believe, but that they do believe in something. People cannot always be put into neat boxes as to what they believe. Asking people about their spiritual and religious needs is not a straightforward tick-box question, but for ease, that is how it often ends up.

So how do we ask about spirituality?

Given the above, it is not at all surprising that many clinicians can find it complex and confusing to ask patients about their spirituality because of the range of definitions and answers that could be given. Unlike other areas of patient care such as pain relief or toileting requirements, there is no set protocol as to how to ask about spiritual or religious needs, and no guidance, matrix or algorithm as to what to do with the response. This can easily lead to the scenario: if you do not want to know the answer, it is best not to ask the question.

The clinicians who have contributed to this volume have found ways to be with their patients in order to find out about what they, the patient, regard as being spiritual, and to use the responses in how they treat their patients. The clinicians know why they bother – because it matters to find out.

How to use this book

Each of the contributors was given the opportunity to write in their own personal style so that they could write from their own very personal experience and reflection. You will find that there are repetitions of references and quotes, and you will find very distinctive and individual styles of writing. You might want to read the book from cover to cover, or you might want to select specific chapters. Either way, you will find a rich diversity of opinion, approach and practice.

Bobbie Farsides lectures in ethics at the Brighton and Sussex Medical School, and is responsible for the training of future doctors, and here she helps us think about the responsibility that professionals have to find out about their own spiritual concerns as well as those of their patients. Many people requiring healthcare will first present to their local GP, and Jo DeBono describes how important it is to find out from patients more than just the physical symptoms, and how these inform what is going on for the patient. Many other people will present with mental health issues, and Tim Ojo and Andy Nuttall, who work in the discipline of mental healthcare, help us understand that for their patients the issues are not physical, and that patients often present as broken spirits.

As a gynaecologist, Peter Larsen-Disney tells us that caring for the whole person is the key to care. This is reflected in Cathy Garland's experience as a neonatal consultant who focuses first on the needs of the baby, but always wants to include parents' needs and what is spiritual to them in order to help the whole family unit. Somnath Mukhopadhyay is chair of paediatrics, and demonstrates the expertise that is required when seeing patients, but also the frustration of not having enough time to explore all their and their families' needs, as he knows this would really help.

Pat Shields offers a frank view of her work, believing it to be difficult for patients who may feel shame and embarrassment to express what is really important to them in order for the clinician to care for them and they for themselves. Patients living with dementia often cannot tell us what is important to them: Muna Al-Jawad's chapter on spirituality and dementia care starts from her view as an atheist, and leads us through her work with patients and teaching with doctors, using her own cartoons and the concept of autobiofictionalography to describe how she cares for her patients.

Caring for patients when there are difficult decisions about which treatment option to choose, which one might be most appropriate for body and soul, is discussed by Adam MacDiarmaid-Gordon in his work with renal patients. Another group for whom it can be difficult to find out what is important, and therefore what the most appropriate way forward might be for, is stroke patients, for whom communication is often not at all easy. Nicola Gainsborough and her team run a stroke unit, and whilst time is of the essence, taking time is also important, and thus staff must be flexible and adaptable to the needs of their patients. The unit completes a form about the needs and wishes of every patient, a copy of which is included at the end of this chapter, which helps to highlight what is 'spiritual' to the patient.

Using forms and assessment tools can be useful for patients who are at the end of life, but as Nigel Spencer and Rachel Reed discuss in their conversation about caring for patients at the end of life, it is so often our own experience and attitude that can give patients and families the ability to talk and share what they regard as being spiritually helpful as life is ending.

References

Brighton and Sussex University Hospitals NHS Trust (2015) *Religion and Belief Policy*. Brighton.

GMC (General Medical Council) (2013) *Good Medical Practice*. Available at www.gmc-uk. org/guidance/good_medical_practice.asp, accessed on 3 January 2017.

Guardian, The (2016) Editorial: *The Guardian view on the Reformation, 500 years on: A force for unity*. 31 October. Available at www.theguardian.com/commentisfree/2016/ oct/31/the-guardian-view-on-the-reformation-500-years-on-a-force-for-unity, accessed on 3 January 2017.

NHS England (2015a) *NHS Chaplaincy Programme*. Available at www2.rcn.org.uk/__data/ assets/pdf_file/0008/372995/003887.pdf, accessed on 3 January 2017.

NHS England (2015b) *NHS Chaplaincy Guidelines 2015: Promoting Pastoral, Spiritual and Religious Care*. Available at www.england.nhs.uk/wp-content/uploads/2015/03/nhs-chaplaincy-guidelines-2015.pdf, accessed on 3 January 2017.

RCN (Royal College of Nursing) (2010) *Spirituality in Nursing Care: A Pocket Guide*. Available at www2.rcn.org.uk/__data/assets/pdf_file/0008/372995/003887.pdf, accessed on 3 January 2017.

RCPsych (Royal College of Psychiatrists) (no date) *Spirituality and Psychiatry Special Interest Group*. Available at www.rcpsych.ac.uk/workinpsychiatry/ specialinterestgroups/spirituality.aspx, accessed on 3 January 2017.

RSA (Royal Society of Arts) (2014) *Spiritualise: Revitalising Spirituality to Address 21st Century Challenges*. Available at www.thersa.org/discover/publications-and-articles/ reports/spiritualise-revitalising-spirituality-to-address-21st-century-challenges, accessed on 3 January 2017.

Sheldrake, P. (2012) *Spirituality: A Very Short Introduction*. Oxford: Oxford University Press.

UKBHC (United Kingdom Board of Healthcare Chaplaincy) (2009) *Standards for Healthcare Chaplaincy Services 2009*. Available at www.ukbhc.org.uk/sites/default/ files/standards_for_healthcare_chapalincy_services_2009.pdf, accessed on 3 January 2017.

1

Spirituality and the Ethics of Professional Responsibility

Bobbie Farsides

Bobbie Farsides, BSc, PhD, is Professor of Clinical and Biomedical Ethics at Brighton and Sussex Medical School. She has a longstanding research interest in the experience of healthcare professionals and scientists working in ethically contested fields of healthcare. Bobbie is also interested in the role that ethics and ethicists can play in the development and implementation of health policy. She is a member of a number of committees, and has twice served as a Specialist Adviser to the House of Lords.

Healthcare professionals have many responsibilities to fulfil in their day-to-day working lives, some of which are literally a matter of life and death, others of which border on the mundane and routinely straightforward. Protocols and guidance have proliferated in recent times, and the checks and balances applied to clinical practice have become more sophisticated and, some would argue, more burdensome. It is against this background that I raise the possibility of a healthcare professional having responsibilities in relation to spiritual matters, be that regarding their own spirituality or that of the people they care for.

We could spend a lot of time disagreeing or indeed attempting to agree on a definition of spirituality, so it is probably best to start with a brief statement of what I think we are talking about. I take a very simple approach to spirituality and present it as our wish to connect with something greater than the world we see around us. It can be about looking for meaning in ways that cannot be explained in terms of the science or bare facts of the matter. In seeking a spiritual experience we may look beyond ourselves and accept guidance from formal religion or organised worldviews, or we may look inwards in a wish to connect with our spiritual selves. We could make the pursuit of spiritual wellbeing a major project in our lives, or we may 'take it when it comes' and cherish a spiritual moment for its unpredictability and fleetingness. A spiritual experience may be tied to any of our senses; it could be profoundly thoughtful and reflective, or it could be visceral and experiential. You could find yourself in a spiritual place because you worked hard to create it or because you simply happened upon it. My spirituality may look very different to yours and may have a very different place in my life.

I would like to begin by thinking about the healthcare professional's own spirituality before considering the role healthcare professionals play in supporting the spiritual needs of their patients. As someone who selects people to enter medical school and then teaches and nurtures them for five years, it is interesting to reflect on whether their spirituality ever comes into consideration. As a selector, I could ask if it is desirable for someone to have a well-developed spiritual identity or a spiritual approach to life when entering medical school. As an educator, I could ask what role if any I might have in relation to developing someone's spirituality and exploring its relevance. Realistically there is little chance during the selection process to explore someone's spiritual identity, but at a medical school that values openness and open-mindedness and weaves ethical reflection through the entire curriculum, one discovers more about students over time including, in some cases, their approach to spiritual matters.

At risk of introducing stereotypes, we can think about Sophie and Dan. Sophie comes to medical school clearly committed to serving the holistic needs of patients. She often talks about the importance of patient narratives and biography, the need to situate medical decisions within the context of more detailed life stories. Her communication skills are such that she soon becomes a go-to person for colleagues wishing to find out more about their patients. She is a great listener and people open up to her. It is unremarkable in a way that Sophie finds herself engaging in discussions about spirituality with some of her patients, because she has the skill of ascertaining what matters to people. Dan is an equally committed young doctor in training, and believes passionately that modern medicine should tend to the soul as well as the body. He has a deep belief in the importance of accessing the spiritual dimension of every patient, and he sometimes feels he has failed when he cannot communicate with people on this level.

Here we have two good people with an interest in spirituality, but maybe Dan, with his intrinsic interest in the subject, has less chance of doing good in a medical setting than Sophie, whose broader interest in what matters to her patients at some fundamental level means spirituality may or may not come up.

If we discover that Sophie has no particular spiritual attachments of her own, we would feel none the worse about her. On the other hand, if we find that Dan sees his entry into medicine as a stage on his own spiritual journey, we might become concerned about his persistence in exploring other people's spiritual experiences because it comes to look like a means to his own ends. Whilst we might admire someone for having a clear interest in developing their spiritual experience and identity, we would want to know that this interest fits with the other demands of the vocational path they have chosen. Addressing one's own spiritual needs cannot take priority, and the project might even need to be put to one side on occasion, especially when professional duties conflict with one's values and beliefs.

One would never want a doctor to become 'spiritually self-indulgent', to adapt a phrase coined by the moral philosopher J.C. Smart, nor would one want someone to see their role as a doctor as a means to offering spiritual enlightenment or guidance. Smart was a consequentialist in his ethical approach, thinking that the way to make moral progress was to consider the consequences of one's actions aiming at the greatest utility (Williams, pp.40–53). It is easy to see how a concern with one's own moral wellbeing or spiritual state could act as a distraction or even a barrier in this moral framework requiring, as it does, that you treat everyone as equal and do not overestimate the utility of your own wellbeing.

On the other hand, if we think that there is merit in giving responsibilities to those best placed to fulfil them, we might say that the person who attends to their own spiritual needs places themselves in a better position to benefit others. So, for example, the person who can accommodate their work within their spiritual framework might be far more effective than the person who struggles to do so. The practitioner who can seek solace or support through their spiritual practices may be better able to cope with the pressures of work and the challenges they face. The person whose own spiritual house is in order may have greater reserves to offer to others. In cases such as these the issue becomes an empirical one of whether the doctor who attends to her own spiritual wellbeing has a better chance of doing good for others. If the answer is yes, we can find space for spiritual development within a consequentialist framework. This, in turn, raises the interesting question of where a professional can turn for support if they are troubled or challenged by spiritual matters. Indeed, we could ask a prior question regarding the extent to which healthcare professionals would feel comfortable seeing such support or expressing such a need.

This aside, the issue seems to be one of balance, finding an Aristotelian-style mean in regard to spirituality as a virtue, finding a habit of behaviour that falls somewhere between being spiritually self-obsessed and being oblivious to the very thought of a spiritual dimension to life. As in so many areas of moral life, the uncontroversial place to rest in terms of a virtue is rarely at an extreme. Consider courage, an excess of which becomes recklessness, which, in a medical context, could be as damaging as timidity or cowardice. Or honesty, which is about so much more than a crude commitment to truth-telling, and will often be about how to present the truth in a way that is consistent with the larger project of looking after someone's health. Similarly, with spirituality, one might not want an individual to be too concerned with piety in the interests of allowing them to function as a doctor.

The interesting thing is that given the possibility of being and doing good things without reference to spirituality, we might at times feel more comfortable with those in whom an interest in spirituality is lacking over those who are impeded by their own spiritual preoccupations.

If commitment to a particular spiritual approach is combined with intolerance or ignorance of any alternative, a healthcare professional may be less able to treat all-comers equally. If one's own spiritual wellbeing always takes precedence when it comes into conflict with aspects of professional duty, there is reason for concern. Whilst we would never want to condone intolerance based on a rejection of spirituality, we should similarly be wary of those who claim a monopoly in terms of spiritual truth and enlightenment. As is often the case, a traditional idiom seems to work well in this context: a place for everything and everything in its place. In modern medicine, we see the space for spirituality in the context of patient-centred holistic care. We are less open to the idea of seeing the practice of medicine as an opportunity for providing, or even offering, spiritual salvation.

There have been several cases in recent years where healthcare professionals and patients have come into conflict when the professional has decided to profess or impose their beliefs in a clinical setting. The cases have ranged over issues such as wearing a religious symbol, offering to pray for patients and enquiring as to the religious beliefs of others in a clinical setting.

The professional guidance arising in the wake of these cases is clear, and our student doctors need to understand them from an early point in their training. In the 2013 document *Personal Beliefs and Medical Practice*, the General Medical Council (GMC 2013a) states:

> We recognise that personal beliefs and cultural practices are central to the lives of doctors and patients, and that all doctors have personal values that affect their day-to-day practice. We don't wish to prevent doctors from practising in line with their beliefs and values, as long as they also follow the guidance in *Good Medical Practice* (2013b). Neither do we wish to prevent patients from receiving care that is consistent with, or meets the requirements of, their beliefs and values.

The document goes on to address in some detail the principles set out in the core GMC document *Good Medical Practice*, where the following statement helpfully introduces the idea of professional boundaries (my emphasis):

Talking to patients about personal beliefs

29. In assessing a patient's conditions and taking a history, you should take account of spiritual, religious, social and cultural factors, as well as their clinical history and symptoms (see *Good Medical Practice* paragraph 15a). It may therefore be appropriate to ask a patient about their personal beliefs. However, you must not put pressure on a patient to discuss or justify their beliefs, or the absence of them.

30. During a consultation, you should keep the discussion relevant to the patient's care and treatment. *If you disclose any personal information to a patient, including talking to a patient about personal beliefs, you must be very careful not to breach the professional boundary that exists between you. These boundaries are essential to maintaining a relationship of trust between a doctor and a patient.*

31. *You may talk about your own personal beliefs only if a patient asks you directly about them, or indicates they would welcome such a discussion. You must not impose your beliefs and values on patients, or cause distress by the inappropriate or insensitive expression of them.*

Reading between the lines and looking at the legislation quoted in the annex to the GMC advice, it is easy to see that it has been written to apply mainly when ethically contested therapies such as termination of pregnancy are being considered. Clearly there is a real potential for a clash of views in this most contested of areas, and some clinicians may feel that the spiritual wellbeing of their patient is under threat if they make a choice that does not sit comfortably with their spiritual identity. On the other hand, a clinician with particular spiritual and/or religious beliefs may feel unable to offer abortion as a therapeutic option, not because of where it will lead the patient, but because of the threat to their own moral integrity.

It could be argued that the traditional commitment to non-directive counselling in obstetrics and the ability to conscientiously object to partake in the provision of abortion mean that the boundary between medical and moral intervention is more carefully protected here than in other areas of medicine. The claim is that women are protected from unwanted incursions into their own moral and spiritual deliberations, and healthcare professionals can 'keep their own hands clean' if their spiritual and/or religious beliefs demand it. In practice, this means that ethically or spiritually focused discussions will be seen as difficult, and to some extent inadvisable, within the clinical setting.

However, there is another side to the story. One might find in fact that some patients would welcome an open-minded discussion with their clinician about the spiritual impact of choices they might be considering. The same might be true of, say, a couple considering what to do with spare embryos created during fertility treatment. Evidence suggests that they could find it difficult to access such a conversation within the clinical environment.

This raises interesting questions for a clinician who recognises this need in a patient but feels personally unable to respond to it. Where can the clinician refer the patient for a discussion that will respect boundaries whilst allowing the patient to explore their own moral and spiritual beliefs? Whilst it is clear that one can 'cause distress by the inappropriate or insensitive expression' (GMC 2013b) of one's views, it is also possible to cause distress by ignoring the spiritual dimension of medical decision-making.

One could argue that as a healthcare professional your job is to establish if and when spiritual needs become relevant to the care of particular patients, and having done so, what can reasonably be done to meet their needs. It is never appropriate to impose your own beliefs or assume the beliefs of another. It might not always be necessary or helpful to start on the path of establishing someone's spiritual beliefs, especially at a point where those needs are trumped by more urgent and serious considerations. However, there will be many situations in which the spiritual beliefs of a person could hold the key to establishing what is or is not in their best interest, and this, in certain circumstances, becomes a fundamental moral and legal duty of healthcare professionals.

So for example, in the context of assisted reproduction or termination of pregnancy, if a patient is clearly identifying themselves as holding religious or spiritual views that will sit uncomfortably with the choices they are exploring, someone may need to ensure that they are given the opportunity at least to explore their preparedness for the possibility of moral conflict. Many years ago, I considered the question of whether you could genuinely consent to the creation, storage, use or disposal of human embryos with your own gametes without first thinking about how you would consider their moral status once they existed. Again, this is an empirical question to which the answer might be different for different people. You could say that it is fairly predictable that those who hold strong spiritual beliefs about the sanctity of human life should consider the impact of treatment on their spiritual wellbeing before embarking upon it. The question is, when and with whom should they do this moral work?

So how do you introduce spirituality into the complex mix of interactions between healthcare professional and patient, particularly when the mantra of non-directiveness tends to push such topics outside the clinic? In attempting to answer this question, an interesting starting point is to ask whose job it is to 'do the spiritual bit'. The role of chaplains is obvious and interesting here, both in terms of their physical presence within the hospital and in terms of how and to whom they present themselves. Yet many would worry about the extent to which the chaplain is genuinely free to offer support and advice given their own spiritual frame of reference. Nonetheless, the chaplain's role gives them particular permissions to enter ethically and spiritually sensitive areas others might avoid. Having said this, their job may not be straightforward.

If you are approached by a person whose professional role clearly encompasses the religious and the spiritual, you will be unsurprised if they question you or invite you to speak on such matters. Those who do not have a strong faith, or indeed any religious views at all, may nonetheless value the opportunity to speak to someone unafraid to probe this area of their experience. Others, however, will feel unable to separate the idea of a formal religious identity from the person standing before them ordained and robed, particularly if they represent a religion the patient has rejected (or felt rejected by). In a city like Brighton and Hove, with an avowedly secular identity, the chaplain may face particular challenges in providing spiritual solace to those who enter the hospital.

Other professional encounters will not be characterised primarily in terms of spiritual care, but it will nonetheless be uncontroversially seen as part of the mix. If you have spent a gentle hour-and-a-half speaking to a community palliative care nurse about your illness, your hopes and fears, your treatment preferences, you may be unsurprised if and when the subject of your spiritual beliefs is explored. Indeed, the World Health Organization (WHO) definition of palliative medicine explicitly acknowledges the duty to provide spiritual care (WHO 2015), and within the discipline Dame Cicely Saunders was quick to alert practitioners to the realities of spiritual pain (Clark 1999). On the other hand, if the topic of spirituality was introduced by your rheumatologist during a pressured outpatient appointment, or it arose whilst you sat waiting for an MRI scan, you would possibly be confused and maybe even unsettled.

This is not to say that there is no place for spirituality in these encounters. If in the care you received in those settings you felt that you had been shown care and respect and you had felt free to express your individuality, you might, in turn, feel minded to reveal something of your spiritual self, be that in your discussion of your condition with your rheumatologist or in your chosen coping mechanisms within the notoriously challenging MRI scanner. Whilst chaplains should expect a proportion of patients to call on them to have just this discussion, and a palliative care nurse may hope that the matter comes up and be prepared to handle it, the rheumatologist might feel surprised and somewhat unskilled in the face of a request to address spiritual concerns, but it is important to allow them to surface.

Before rushing in and suggesting that all medical specialities need to be equipped to discuss spiritual concerns with their patients, one might consider whether on some occasions the patient's introduction of a spiritual dimension to a consultation is a proxy for broader concerns. It may be that the patient is actually asking a disguised question about diagnosis and prognosis. It may, in some senses, be a 'test' of the trust that is seen as so important in the GMC guidance. Behind a statement or question about spirituality a patient could be saying, 'If I tell you who I am and what matters to me, can I trust you to take that seriously?' 'When I tell you I'm struggling with the idea of heaven and hell, can you hear that I'm also considering my mortality?' 'When you raise your eyes because I say I want to place my faith in the healing power of nature and the spiritual world, can you not understand what that says about my treatment experiences so far?' The willingness to have a conversation about ostensibly spiritual issues might be the first step to ensuring that a patient retains trust in their clinician at a point when they are struggling with some of the hardest aspects of their illness or disease. It might also allow the clinician to feel on firmer ground as the non-spiritual back story is revealed, and without ignoring or sweeping the spiritual element of the conversation away, the clinicians nonetheless find themselves in safer territory.

It is important to remember that being given access to someone's spiritual beliefs is a privilege and an act of trust. In marking our difference we sometimes make ourselves vulnerable. In clearly stating our identity we hope for acceptance but understand that we may meet rejection. A commitment to ensuring that people feel safe to assert publicly their spiritual and religious identities in non-coercive ways is a hallmark of a liberal and inclusive society. When patients feel safe to present themselves to a healthcare professional whilst displaying clear and unambiguous markers of their beliefs, they are trusting (or at least hoping) that they will be accepted and treated in a non-prejudicial manner. If a healthcare professional feels safe to do the same, they are saying 'I trust you to judge me on my talents and the way that I treat you, not in terms of (what you assume to be) my beliefs.' Thus the simple fact that an institution or wider society allows for the presence of religious and spiritual diversity might be a spiritual act in itself. We should work towards a world in which people will find solace in heterogeneity and feel safe in a space where many different types of people have come to rest.

As I write this at the beginning of 2017, it feels hugely important to protect and enrich our spiritual selves. As I said at the outset, some of us will seek help to do this whilst others will struggle and/or triumph alone. One might be tempted still to ask what place a hospital and the staff within it have to play in this. In trying to answer that question, I end up minded of the idea of a hospital as a refuge or sanctuary, a place we find ourselves in (rarely willingly) with important work to do, be that living well or dying well, a place where people should be able to come and feel free to bare their bodies and their souls, a place where people are removed from everyday life and forced, through illness and in the interests of recovery, or in preparation for death, to spend time away from that which so readily distracts us from the spiritual. It should be possible to make a hospital a place where important spiritual work is undertaken, but in order for this to be a reality as opposed to a dream, we have to work at the level of institutions and individuals to create a culture that is accepting and respectful of the variety of spiritual perspectives that will be revealed. We have to appreciate that the work involved in diagnosing and responding to spiritual pain and suffering will be challenging and may feel even more uncertain in terms of what it can achieve than modern medicine. Some patients won't want their care to touch on the spiritual, others will directly request explicit forms of spiritual support, and yet others will be at an early stage of recognising and articulating their own needs. The trick, as ever, is reading the signs, something we try to instil in our medical students from day one. Look, listen, be open to what you see and hear, and learn to recognise when a patient is asking for something that will address their spiritual needs as well as, or instead of, the other more medically defined goals that they and their carers are pursuing together. So we return to Sophie and Dan and maybe understand a little better what we are looking to nurture in our future doctors.

References

Clark, D. (1999) '"Total pain", disciplinary power and the body in the work of Cicely Saunders, 1958–1967.' *Social Science and Medicine* 49, 727–736.

GMC (General Medical Council) (2013a) *Personal Beliefs and Medical Practice*. Available at www.gmc-uk.org/Good_practice_in_prescribing.pdf_58834768.pdf, accessed on 7 February 2017.

GMC (2013b) *Good Medical Practice*. Available at www.gmc-uk.org/guidance/good_medical_practice.asp, accessed on 3 January 2017.

Smart, J.J.C. and Williams, B. (1973) *Utilitarianism: For and Against It*. Cambridge: Cambridge University Press.

Williams, B. (1981) *Moral Luck*. Cambridge: Cambridge University Press.

WHO (World Health Organization) (2015) *WHO Definition of Palliative Care*. Available at www.who.int/cancer/palliative/definition/en/, accessed on 7 February 2017.

2

General Practice

THE SOUL OF THE MATTER

Josephine DeBono

Dr Josephine DeBono, BM, DRCOG, MRCGP, qualified in medicine from the University of Southampton in 1982. She has been a general practitioner for 30 years. She is married and has a son and a daughter.

Unsurprisingly, there is no single, widely agreed definition of 'spirituality'. It may refer to almost any kind of activity through which a person seeks meaning, and this may or may not be sacred. It may also refer to personal growth or 'an encounter with one's own spiritual dimension'. Some studies report a positive correlation between spirituality and mental wellbeing, both in healthy and ill people. For the purposes of this chapter, I have tried to simplify the definition as, 'that which most matters to a person'. The General Medical Council (GMC), in its rulebook *Good Medical Practice* (GMC 2013), stipulates that 'a doctor *must* take account of patients' psychological, spiritual, social and cultural factors, their views and values'. Moreover, it also states, 'you (the clinician) must not discriminate against patients by allowing your personal views to affect the treatments that you provide or arrange'.

I have been a general practitioner (GP) for over 30 years. During that time I have worked as a 'sessional' doctor, providing locum cover to a number of practices. I have been a partner in the same practice for 23 years, the last six as senior partner.

Although primary medical services in the UK are currently in a state of some flux, by far the majority of these services are still provided by individual practices that operate essentially as small businesses, contracted to the NHS in order to provide a core set of services, plus any additional services that may have been agreed upon, for example, diabetes care, asthma and so on. This is what most people mean when they say 'general practice'; people are usually registered with a practice in their area, see the same set of clinicians, and thereby develop a therapeutic relationship with these people. This relationship sometimes lasts for decades.

For a variety of perfectly valid reasons this model, although it has worked extremely well since the inception of the National Health Service (NHS) in 1948, has, in the long run, proven to be unsustainable. Small practices are risking becoming unviable and are seeking to merge into ever-larger organisations, thus risking losing the special doctor–patient relationship of the past.

Over 90 per cent of all contacts within the NHS occur in general practice. The average member of the public sees a GP six times a year. For people aged 85 years and over, that figure is more than doubled. There are approximately one million consultations taking place in primary care every single day, and at least 60 per cent of these are estimated to be GP contacts.

Eighteen million people, about a quarter of the population of the UK, are reckoned to have a 'chronic condition'. The vast majority of these people are managed in the community by GPs. These usually work in partnership with other doctors and lead the wider 'primary specific practices'. I cannot emphasise enough the importance of the role that receptionists and telephonists have in delivering patient care and generally influencing the patient experience. They are usually the first point of contact for people, and their attitude and behaviour makes a huge difference to both.

It is extremely important to maintain and develop good access to general practice. This matters both to the patient and to the health system itself. Poor access can cause unnecessary stress and frustration at a time when a person may already be worried. It can also prolong discomfort or pain. Providing good access to the most appropriate clinician is an ever-changing challenge. Much depends on the demographic of the patient population. A relatively young and healthy population is more likely to present with acute conditions that may require on-the-day attention. An older population that is likely to be less mobile usually prefers appointments that can be booked in advance. There is also a noticeable variation between the seasons, with many more acute requests in the winter months.

On average, most GPs will have between 30 and 40 face-to-face consultations a day, about 10 consultations on the telephone plus a variable number of home visits (National Audit Office 2015). There is, of course, much care that is not delivered face-to-face; for example, issuing prescriptions, interpreting pathology results, reading clinic correspondence and any actions that these necessitate.

The older the patient, the more likely they will value continuity of care. At least two thirds of people with a long-term condition say that they have a 'preferred GP'. This figure rises to 75 per cent if the person has a mental health condition at any age, or is aged 75 years or over.

All this puts general practice in an excellent situation to deliver and develop truly fruitful therapeutic relationships. General practice is often the 'intermediary' or translator, in the widest sense, for people who are being investigated or treated in secondary care. It is my experience that people still view hospitals as large, busy, somewhat impersonal places where doctors and nurses are very involved in doing important things. As often as not, after a consultation with a hospital specialist, a person will come to the GP, usually with a list, in order to discuss matters further – questions such as, 'What exactly is meant by this term or phrase?' and so on. This has become more frequent since the advent of patient inclusion in clinical correspondence, and is usually followed by the most difficult question of all, 'But what do *you* think?' My practice is usually to turn the query back to them and to ask them directly at that point what the big issues are for them.

Patients worry about what we all worry about:

- Is it serious?
- Who will look after my children/elderly parents/pets?
- Is this illness likely to change me, and how?

The concept of patient-centred care

Patient-centred care is, or should be, a core value in general practice. There is no agreed definition, although it is generally accepted that the person who is being treated needs to be central to any decision taken regarding their health. There has been much written about this, but essentially it boils down to the fact that a person's views, goals and beliefs need to be taken into account at all times. *The NHS Constitution for England* (Department of Health 2009) states that NHS services *must* reflect the needs and preferences of patients, their families and carers. The Health and Social Care Act (2012) imposes a legal duty on NHS England and Clinical Commissioning Groups to involve patients in their care.

The concept of patient-centred care, therefore, is dependent on clinicians having a good understanding of what really matters to the person in front of them. This ensures that the relationship between the two parties becomes a partnership. This concept comes to the fore in supporting people with long-term conditions to manage their health. There is some evidence that this also improves clinical outcomes. When people are supported in this, they are less likely to use emergency services and they are more likely to stick to their treatment plans, and so on. True patient-centred care is therefore also beneficial to the NHS.

General practice prides itself on its capacity for treating a person 'holistically'. I suspect that this term means different things to different people. I happen to believe that it should mean an understanding of the whole person, body, mind and spirit, as each of these impacts on the other.

Everybody is familiar with the idea of psychosomatic symptoms – in brief, psychological issues that present themselves in a physical form such as rashes, palpitations and some forms of headache. These symptoms can be very difficult to interpret and diagnosis may take more than one consultation. In extreme cases, some people undergo extensive investigations before they are diagnosed appropriately. It is time well spent to ask a few basic questions regarding emotional wellbeing at every consultation as it may avoid many expensive, invasive and unpleasant procedures. Needless to say, this sort of questioning has to be done sensitively and in the right circumstances. However, in my experience, the vast majority of people are more than willing to discuss matters that are important to them with a clinician who cares enough to listen.

First patient story

In September 2004, after years of the nightmare known only to those who live with addiction, my alcoholic ex-husband died in my arms. He was 49 years old. It took 48 long hours from when his ventilator was switched off. I was devastated.

Our GP was surprised when I turned up in his office. He'd never had any insight into my suffering. It had been so long since I'd seen him he didn't realise I was still registered. His main concern was to defend his actions, or rather lack of, leading up to my husband's collapse. I assume he thought I was there for a fight. He was wrong. I was devastated. I left even more so, since he would only prescribe an antidepressant that I had reacted badly to some years before.

It was then I first met Dr DeBono, who took time to really understand me, and all that had happened. I immediately felt I was in safe hands. She diagnosed the mutually re-enforcing trio of stress, depression and insomnia, but was confident if we could improve just one, the others would follow. This did not prove easy with my intolerance to antidepressants. I tried several times over the years, finally vowing 'never again' when my liver rebelled and I turned yellow.

Life just kept happening. Then came the words that I will never forget as Dr DeBono reassured me, 'I will not leave you orphan.'

This biblical saying sums up the essence and importance of spiritual care within healthcare. There is not a drug or easy answer for every medical problem. Each individual, their situation and response to treatment, is unique. Spiritual care means caring enough to take the time to really get to know a patient and what is important to them, way beyond 'holistically': developing a rapport through empathy and compassion, especially in cases of debilitating chronic ill health, where there is little hope of cure but only of improvement; being prepared to be alongside and accessible, so that the individual no longer feels so alone, misunderstood, hopeless and in danger of entering a downward spiral of compounding conditions. Sometimes spiritual care is the only care there is to give. It is always the most important. In my experience, such a level of total patient care is rare because of the time constraints placed on doctors and what it demands of them personally.

I was always greeted as a friend and given more than the time I felt I needed. Dr DeBono wanted to know the whole picture – how was the family, work, and so on? I was always grateful and never took this for granted. I was amazed to find from the NHS feedback website that she seemingly achieved this for all her patients. I will never understand how. The timing of the next appointment was usually stated and often booked on leaving. Because I knew that if I was desperate, and she was available, Dr DeBono would contact me as soon as she could, this only happened once. She was always open to me trying different things as I frantically researched to find something, anything, that would help.

Our faith was important to us both and that gave our particular relationship a deeper spiritual dimension. We both knew there was a power greater than the two of us involved and that was a great comfort to me. Dr DeBono would always ask for my prayers for herself and a particular person who was suffering. This ensured I would always count my blessings, feel less inadequate, and that the relationship was more equal, if there was something I could do to help.

I don't see myself as unique or particularly unfortunate in all this. Variations on both my story and my symptoms are endemic, especially amongst women of a certain age who apparently 'love too much'. The body is not built to keep running permanently on the adrenalin needed to fuel modern life. Eventually something has to give. For me it was my mental health and my thyroid gland, some of the many life-limiting 'hidden disabilities' that receive scant understanding or sympathy. The toughest part was the hostility I faced from members of my own family for my 'lack of effort' when I could not meet their needs or expectations.

Dr DeBono believed me and believed in me. She came to know me well enough to know when I needed a gentle push or permission to give up the struggle and rest for a while. When things were at their worst, she promised me, 'we will get through this'. Not 'you', but 'we'. I didn't quite see how, but finally prayers were answered. I was offered a job on a self-employed basis, so that I could work the hours I could manage and be flexible during what was to be the last year of mum's life. Gradually, rung by rung, I pulled myself out of the slough of despond as my hours, health and self-esteem began to improve.

Had it not been for the spiritual care I received from the wonderful GP who was prepared to shine her own light to journey through the darkness with me, things could have been very different.

I have come across people who have declined certain treatments because that would mean spending a night in hospital away from a beloved pet. Others have a fatalistic attitude towards their illness – 'what will be will be'. This attitude is always worth exploring further as it may have many different meanings – denial of the reality facing them or a true belief in predestination. One of the most fascinating aspects of the GP's job is to observe different people's reactions to what appears to be the same diagnosis. Reactions can vary from straight acceptance to downright denial and everything in between. In such cases, it is crucial to explore such reactions and to 'work' with the person. This is especially true in the case of a serious diagnosis in a relatively young person. It goes without saying that what may be an acceptable prognosis to an 80-year-old is not so to a person half their age.

The management of the, initially, same condition in different people can therefore vary enormously. Nowhere is the saying more apt than 'knowledge is power', and finding out what matters to a person becomes important. Sometimes what matters most is not obvious. As clinicians, we often foolishly assume that we know what is important about a certain condition and its management. We must always stay vigilant so as not to fall into the trap of reflecting our own assumptions onto the patient. This is, in my opinion, where effective teamwork in its broadest sense comes into its own. Patients in general practice, especially those living with a long-term condition requiring multiple attendances, will have come into contact with a wide range of team members, clinical and administrative. I have learned much over the years by observing these encounters as they happen. Ancillary staff also need to be given 'permission' to voice their thoughts and opinions. People often get to know receptionists by their first name, and will often discuss other aspects of their lives that may have a bearing on their clinical condition but that they may not have deemed important enough to tell the doctor. I have learned much from my receptionists who have given me a different insight into why a patient may have been behaving in a certain way.

It is estimated that as much as 40 per cent of all consultations in general practice include an element of mental health. With this group of people, it is even more important to be wide open to any and all clues relating to their inner life. Depression and anxiety are two of the most common conditions that we come across. Counselling services vary across the country, and waiting times for these are long. Locally, specialist mental health services only appear to deal with acute serious mental illness. The GP, therefore, is at the forefront of managing these conditions in the majority of the chronically ill. Here it is even more important to establish a relationship of mutual trust that encompasses all the relevant issues. Again, this will almost never happen at a first consultation, and the clinician therefore needs to ensure that the person will return at a later date. We do not have a recall system in primary care for these people, so it is my practice to ask them to make a subsequent appointment before they leave. I also ensure that the details are stored on their phone or written down, and make sure that a text reminder is sent nearer the time. Some people in this group may be extremely distressed but it is vital that they know that first, there is a plan and, more importantly, that second, somebody has listened and has taken their issues on board.

Second patient story

In January 2009, following a decade of chronic endometriosis that had spread throughout my pelvic cavity and finally into the large bowel, I had an ileostomy. I was 44 years old and, as far as I was concerned, my life as an active wife and mother was over. My head told me that it was the right thing to do and the only option left, but my heart seemed to be full of overwhelming feelings of a lack of confidence, self-esteem, femininity and the fear that my husband couldn't possibly find me attractive ever again. Nearly eight years on, and I can honestly say that it was the best thing that I could have had done. I am fit, healthy, just as active, wearing whatever I want and continuing to enjoy a full relationship with my husband. The scars have healed and my stoma and I have a healthy respect for one another!

Looking back and reflecting on the event and the circumstances that led to it, my GP's ability to see the 'whole me' was, I believe, essential to my recovery. The physical details of the surgery and 'replumbing' went over my head after a while, and I felt I was at saturation point when it came to reading about it. However, my GP's practice of starting every consultation with the question, 'So, how are you doing today?' enabled me to articulate the emotional issues that mattered to me most at that point. When I railed against it with a 'why me?', she didn't give me a rundown of the physical state of my gut but listened, passed me tissues and ignored the allocated appointment time. As a person of faith, I came to see her not just as my doctor but as a friend who was walking alongside me on this fairly rough part of my life's journey.

We now live in a different part of the country, and I enjoy a very good relationship with my current GP. During the past year, I have faced the second biggest challenge of my life. I was made redundant out of the blue and within three months was unemployed for the first time in my adult working life. The scars that I thought had healed completely seven years ago hadn't. They were still there, just scabbed over, and the feelings of no confidence, lack of self-esteem, failure and only being fit for the scrap heap bubbled up to the surface and overflowed. On a routine visit to my GP not long after I had been given news of my redundancy, she simply asked, 'How are things going?' and five minutes later I stopped crying. The physical ailment I had gone about was forgotten, and we talked about how I felt emotionally and spiritually. As a person of faith herself, she understood the effects of losing a job that one regards as one's vocation. I was signed off work for two weeks and told that I was to rest and give myself a chance to regain some of my emotional strength without the stress of going into work for the notice period. I left the surgery thinking, 'Dr J gets it'. The 'whole me' mattered and was being looked after. I continued to see her regularly over the next four to five months, just to check how things were, to talk and to be reassured that what I felt was perfectly natural and that I wasn't going mad. On one occasion as I was going she said she would pray for me and I believed her. And I certainly said a prayer of thanksgiving for her.

The connection between physical illness and one's emotional state is well documented and not for me to discuss here. However, for those who have any kind of spiritual belief, there is an extra dimension. Those who follow the Abrahamic faiths believe that they are made in the image of God and that their life – and all life – is sacred. Thus, the GP's care of the 'whole person' is exactly that: not just the treatment of physical symptoms, but the walking alongside someone for whom the physical symptoms might just be the tip of the iceberg and all they have believed in is being challenged. For those who are terminally ill, it will be sharing with them in that end of life stage and understanding the importance of a 'good death'. The GP is everyone's first port of call, and their opening words can make the difference between sink or swim for the patient. I swam, largely due to the efforts of two remarkable GPs.

This is where I think that the introduction of care plans has a value. It is important that the plan is owned by the person who also owns their condition. The task of the healthcare professional is very much to enable the person to manage the condition, and in order for that to happen, one must know what it is that matters most. At the other end of the spectrum, finding out what matters is important even in a relatively non-complicated physical condition such as osteoarthritis. A person who does not like hospitals will not appreciate a referral, even if clinically that may be the correct thing to do. This is the time when it will be fruitful to find out why and to work with that. Older people especially may have different priorities to younger people, and often have their reasons for choosing one management plan over another.

In general practice, we are faced on a regular basis with people who present with medically unexplained symptoms. The paucity of a known aetiology in these cases can make for a difficult consultation, and most of us learn to tread very carefully. The received wisdom is that there is usually a psychological cause for this type of presentation. However, some people may reject such an explanation. In my experience, it helps to be honest with the person, although one's choice of words is crucial. These symptoms are very real to the patient, even if all investigations have drawn a blank. Believing that these symptoms are real to the patient is a good first step. It is then up to the clinician to ask as many open questions, in as gentle a way as possible, in order to paint the fullest picture of that person as a whole. It is also important to point out that there is much in medicine that we do not understand, and that the door is always open for them to discuss their symptoms again if they wish. I have no problem with saying 'I do not know', if that is the case.

How to achieve this? A cursory view of the literature reveals that there are many different ways of conducting a clinical consultation in general practice. Each has its merits. However, all recommend active listening and encouraging the person to tell their own story. This means listening attentively without interruption, and facilitating both verbal and non-verbal responses. Sometimes silence is appropriate, sometimes repetition or interpretation of a statement. It is important to be alert to non-verbal clues. This goes for both parties – body language, the siting of seats, facial expressions – these all have a part to play. Above all, one needs to allow time, probably the most precious commodity during a busy surgery. One must learn to prioritise. This is not always easy to achieve. Over the years, I have found that sometimes it is a good idea to schedule extra-curricular sessions, outside the routine surgery times or sometimes at the end of one, so that the pressure on time is reduced. This investment has yielded dividends, both to the patient and to me, as it has allowed me to understand better the whole picture, thus making clinical management much less complicated.

I have also learned that it is sometimes necessary to take a more direct approach, using questions such as, 'What are you really bothered about?' I have yet to meet the person who has objected to this approach. The trick is to choose the questions properly at the beginning! Most people are relieved and indeed grateful to have issues spelled out to them and fears voiced. Sometimes saying what most matters is difficult, especially if one has never been asked the question before.

GPs learn to live with uncertainty on a daily basis. Symptoms are not always clear-cut and neither are diagnoses. Again, it has always paid to be honest. Discussing uncertainty and finding a way to manage it requires much work around the person's beliefs and values. I never cease to be in awe of people's resilience and acceptance of sometimes serious medical conditions. This resilience is no doubt mostly attributable to their beliefs and values. I have learned much from patients in this regard.

Third patient story

I was diagnosed with severe depression in October 2015, but, of course, on reflection, I had been depressed for quite a while. The final straw came when I was bullied at work, resulting in a major anxiety attack on my daily commute. I called my GP in quite a state and was seen the same day.

It was a shock to be told I was severely depressed. I was prescribed antidepressants, referred to Time to Talk, signed off work and given a follow-up appointment for the next week. It is important to note that the appointment wasn't rushed in any way, and although I don't recall everything my GP told me, she took her time talking me through the diagnosis. I'm not sure the folk in the waiting room were too impressed, but I was, and always will be, so grateful for her gentle and thoughtful approach.

So now I was sitting at home or, I should say, sleeping at home a good deal of the time. I became very reclusive. The result was:

I stopped going to church.

I stopped reading the Daily Readings for Mass, Morning and Evening Prayer.

I stopped praying.

I stopped doing housework.

Personal care slipped down my priorities.

So on the one hand I was physically and mentally cared for and the drugs certainly alleviated the anxiety. My family were very supportive, but the empty feeling remained. I can only describe that empty feeling as a great pain that weighed me down. Time to Talk made initial contact and put me on a waiting list for CBT (Cognitive Behavioural Therapy).

The CBT was helpful as it made me get out of the house and gave me some good coping mechanisms. It also made me realise I wasn't alone. The whole push was to get back to work and functioning again, which is a positive thing, and I started a phased return to work, being back full time in the January. Deep down I knew something was still wrong. I had lost something and I struggled. By June I was signed off again, still with that pain.

I slept a lot for the first week and it was at this point I thought, 'I can't go on like this and something has to change.' My monthly Magnificat (Mass and prayers for the month) had arrived in the post. This was the turning point. I'm ashamed to say I drove the mile to church, whereas in oridnary circumstances I would've walked, and I sneaked in at the back and attended Mass. If you don't have faith, it's hard to explain. It wasn't an overnight cure in any way, but the pain eased during Mass. I was able to pray a little, and I could just sit and be still in mind and body. I do not know what I asked for, but a healing had begun. I was the prodigal daughter returned, and I was welcomed by God and a lot of noisy parishioners who wanted to know why I wasn't at work and was I okay? They were so kind to me.

Now, of course, it's not that easy, and regaining my daily prayer rhythm was and is still challenging. I am a bit of a nomad when it comes to Mass. Sometimes I need anonymity as I can't deal with people. It's the same on my commute. I choose to travel early and avoid the crush, and I choose to go to a different church so I can sit and be still. The pain can appear at unexpected times, but I still myself and concentrate and say a Hail Mary (14 seconds). It works. My faith and the love of God sustains me. Importantly I'm not alone or isolated. I feel God's presence in my life. I don't always acknowledge it as I should, but it's there, a grace that I do not always deserve.

During this time, I've learned a lot of things about myself and I've become more accepting. I enjoy simple things such as the sun on my face, the trees turning gold. Maybe I just notice them more, but they make me happy. My relationships with friends and family have changed. I am more open with them and so these relationships have grown into something richer.

I don't fool myself, like a diabetic or an alcoholic. I think depression will be something that is always there, but I have God with me. So, in the words of Julian of Norwich, 'All will be well, and shall be well and all manner of things shall be well.'

For the moment I am off the antidepressants, but I wouldn't hesitate to take them again if needed. I am not turning my back on medicine. I just believe there is more than one way to receive healing.

Again, I cannot emphasise enough the need to be non-judgemental. Some people have beliefs and values that may be alien to the clinician. Some people also put much faith in alternative or complementary therapies. Whatever one may think of these various interventions, if they matter to the person in front of you, they need to matter to you. There is only one exception to this rule and that is if, clinically, you feel that the person's beliefs are causing them harm.

A GP learns to make good use of any and every opportunity to learn about their patients. For this reason, I have never been a fan of the 'one issue per appointment' rule. Time and time again people have presented with something relatively trivial only to divulge, in passing, something that has potentially serious repercussions or that may have been the real reason for their visit. 'While I am here, doctor' happens frequently. This is especially true in the case of most men who, as a rule, do not attend unless pressed and who are reticent about admitting to any issues that are not physical.

I feel that I need to make a special mention of counselling regarding termination of pregnancy. The GP is usually the first professional meeting for these patients, and the consultation is, unfortunately in many cases, probably the only occasion where a discussion about this important decision is had. This is the time to listen to the woman about what it is that she wants and why. For most women, this is a confusing, bewildering and frightening time. It is important to explore their values and beliefs as, whatever decision they make, their life will be changed and therefore, whatever choice they make has to be right for them. It is preferable to see them on their own as this allows for a more open discussion. Again, the virtues of listening and not passing judgement cannot be overestimated.

References

DH (Department of Health) (2009) *The NHS Constitution for England*. London: DH. Available at http://webarchive.nationalarchives.gov.uk/+/www.dh.gov.uk/en/publicationsandstatistics/publications/publicationspolicyandguidance/dh_093419, accessed on 2 March 2017.

GMC (General Medical Council) (2013) *Good Medical Practice*. Available at www.gmc-uk.org/guidance/good_medical_practice.asp, accessed on 7 February 2017.

Health and Social Care Act (2012). Available at www.legislation.gov.uk/ukpga/2012/7/contents/enacted, accessed on 7 February 2017.

National Audit Office (2015) *Stocktake of Access to General Practice in England HC605*. Available at www.nao.org.uk/report/stocktake-of-access-to-general-practice-in-england, accessed on 7 February 2017.

3

Mental Health

PART 1: MINDING THE SPIRIT

Tim Ojo

Dr Tim Ojo, MBBS, MSc, MBA, FRCPsych, FInstLM, FSFFMLM, Diploma in Executive Coaching, is a consultant psychiatrist with many years' experience of clinical practice and medical management. For seven years he was Executive Medical Director of Sussex Partnership NHS Foundation Trust. He is an experienced executive coach and leadership mentor, an accredited mediator, and was in the first cohort of senior founding Fellows of the Faculty of Medical Leadership and Management, as well as being a Fellow of the Royal College of Psychiatrists and a Fellow of the Institute of Leadership & Management.

Preamble

I come to this endeavour as a psychiatrist with an active Christian faith that is unapologetically ecumenical in nature. I have been exposed to a number of other faith traditions through friendships, my upbringing and contact with observant patients. I am aware that psychiatry as a profession has at times had a disputatious relationship with religious and spiritual worldviews. I have written this with the express intent of being a bit detached and matter-of-fact, mainly to make it useful to clinicians with or without belief.

Outline and context

Mental healthcare, to a greater or lesser extent, is concerned with the alleviation of human suffering. Mental illness frequently affects the equilibrium of human existence adversely, causing distress and disturbance. So in the hospitals, outpatient clinics, inpatient wards, community bases and rehabilitation units across the country, men and women bring their unique yet universal stories and experiences to the attention of professionals. They seek alleviation of their discomfort and restoration of their wellbeing and mental stability.

Psychiatry is one of the professions concerned with attending to the needs of those with mental ill health. Psychiatrists work by gathering salient information from the patient (history taking), assessing the mental state, formulating a diagnosis and proposing a course of treatment, pharmacological or otherwise. Psychiatrists are doctors who have chosen to specialise in the treatment of mental illness and in doing so encounter dimensions of human experience that go beyond the boundaries of bodily symptoms. Indeed, the various disordered beliefs, abnormal auditory or visual perceptions, and fluctuations of mood that define major mental illness often enough give rise to existential questions that are profoundly spiritual in nature.

These questions are frequently overlooked and underexplored in this modern era of neuroscience-dominated psychiatric practice. It is against this background that I will share my approach to dealing with the spiritual dimensions of mental healthcare. In the over 20 years that I have been practising psychiatry, it has become increasingly obvious to me and other practitioners that addressing the spiritual needs of individual patients makes for better quality clinical care.

Spiritual needs in mental health

The Royal College of Psychiatrists, in a leaflet entitled 'Spirituality and Mental Health' (2014), gives a broad definition of spirituality based on the notion that it is something everyone can experience. Spirituality in essence helps to give meaning and purpose to the things we value, can provide hope and healing in the face of loss and suffering, and provides the impetus to seek the best relationship with ourselves, with others and with the future.

Chris Cook (2004) gives a rounded definition of spirituality as:

> ...a distinctive, potentially creative, and universal dimension of human experience arising both within the inner subjective awareness of individuals and within communities, social groups and traditions. It may be experienced as a relationship with that which is intimately 'inner', imminent and personal, within the self and others, and/or as relationship with that which is wholly 'other', transcendent and beyond the self. It is experienced as being of fundamental or ultimate importance and is thus concerned with matters of meaning and purpose in life, truth, and values. (2004, pp.548-549)

Against that background it is abundantly clear that recognising the role spirituality plays in recovery from mental illness is imperative. Indeed, one might go so far as to contend that elucidation of the spiritual needs of patients is indicative of high-quality psychiatric care. The Mental Health Foundation (2007) appears to concur with the assertions above in their view that:

> ...spirituality can help people maintain good mental health. It can help them cope with everyday stress and can keep them grounded. Tolerant and inclusive spiritual communities can provide valuable support and friendship. There is some evidence of links between spirituality and improvements in people's mental health, although researchers do not know exactly how this works.

They go on to describe how mental healthcare can demonstrably respond to the spiritual needs of patients by:

- acknowledging spirituality in people's lives
- providing opportunities for service users and staff to talk about spirituality
- encouraging service users to tell staff their needs
- helping service users to express their spirituality

- using person-centred planning and incorporating spiritual needs
- giving service users and staff opportunities to talk about spirituality.

(based on The Mental Health Association 2007)

Motivation for asking about spiritual needs

The central motivation for a practitioner asking about the spiritual needs of a patient must be to gain a better holistic understanding of the patient's context. Ideally this understanding should form the basis of compassionate and empowering mental healthcare. In reality, psychiatry and spirituality, whether of the religious or non-religious variety, have a complicated and contentious relationship. Harold Koenig (2008) reminds us that studies show the widespread prejudice of UK, US and Canadian psychiatrists against religion and its limited integration into psychiatric assessments. Nevertheless, Cook (2013, p.3, para. 1), in a position paper for the Royal College of Psychiatrists, is unequivocal in asserting 'the value of considering spirituality and religion as a part of good clinical practice'. He goes on to state that guidance is required to 'ensure that matters of spirituality and religion are not avoided in clinical practice when in fact they may need to be addressed for the benefit of the patient, but at the same time to ensure that a patient's lack of religious or spiritual beliefs is equally respected' (Cook 2013, p.3, para. 2). Therefore, it behoves mental health practitioners to develop the proficiency necessary to integrate their knowledge of the spiritual dimensions of a given patient's life into helping them recover from illness. This proficiency takes time and training to develop, and in the next section an exploration of helpful professional guidance is undertaken.

Professional guidance on asking patients about spiritual needs

Good psychiatric practice requires that a psychiatrist be competent in obtaining a full and relevant history, which includes social and cultural factors. It further requires that 'a psychiatrist must provide care that does not discriminate and is sensitive to issues of gender, ethnicity, colour, culture, lifestyle, beliefs, sexual orientation, age and disability' (Cook 2013, p.4, para. 1). And again, 'when negotiating the aims and outcomes of treatment plans, a psychiatrist must recognise and respect the diversity of patients' lifestyles, including cultural issues, religious and spiritual beliefs, ambitions and personal goals' (Cook 2013, p.4, para. 2).

Culliford (2007) reminds us that taking a spiritual history requires an 'empathic engagement' with the patient, which requires the judicious use of both 'intuition and initiative'. He goes on to recommend a gentle unhurried approach that may require more than one conversation. However, he is also clear that sometimes a rapid evaluation may be required in some cases based on the mental state of the given patient and other relevant contextual factors. He recommends the use of two 'screening questions' as follows:

1. Are you particularly religious or spiritual?
2. What helps you most when things are difficult or hard?

These questions help to open up the possibility of further exploration of the beliefs and values that give meaning to the lives of patients. Additionally, more structured frameworks exist to assist in capturing the required information.

Pulchaski and Romer (2000) provide the mnemonic FICA, which any healthcare professional could use to good effect. FICA, broken into its component parts, is as follows:

- **F**aith and belief (what gives the patient's life meaning)
- **I**mportance (how important this is to their situation)
- **C**ommunity (their place in any social or religious group)
- **A**ddress in care (how they would like their beliefs to be addressed in their healthcare).

Another helpful framework is the HOPE questions by Anandarajah and Hight (2001). Their mnemonic helps the assessor to focus on four themes as follows:

- Sources of **H**ope – meaning, strength, comfort and connection
- **O**rganised religion
- **P**ersonal spirituality and practices
- **E**ffects on medical, psychiatric and end of life issues.

The information gathered from the spiritual assessment should be integrated into other parts of the psycho-bio-social assessment, to give a comprehensive psycho-bio-socio-spiritual assessment of the patient. If done sensitively, properly and thoroughly, the patient's engagement and trust in the therapeutic alliance is strengthened.

The best way to increase a practitioner's competence in undertaking bio-psycho-social-spiritual assessments is habitually to use any of the frameworks discussed above as part of their routine. Clearly the practitioner's belief or lack of it should not impair their willingness to assess spirituality as long as they are prepared for the variety of responses they are likely to encounter. As stated earlier, an absence of any spiritual inclination in individual patients should never be an issue in itself.

From theory to practice: dealing with the spirituality of patients

In practice, it is often the case that a straightforward assessment of spirituality may not be possible due to the mental state or level of arousal of the patient. At other times the presenting complaints of the patient involve religious or spiritual themes, thus necessitating immediate further exploration. In this section I illustrate the varied ways in which the issue of spirituality could arise in the course of everyday clinical practice with three vignettes from my clinical experiences over the years. I endeavour to focus on the core issues and limit identifiability.

The prayerful man

In the mid-1990s, as a registrar in South London working with a rapid assessment team, I was called to assess a man in his 20s who had refused to break his fast during Ramadan. His behaviour leading up to the request for an assessment had been excessively pious, and he had been praying far more than the prescribed five times a day, in a noisy manner. Recognising that his spiritual and religious beliefs were clearly very important to him, on the way to assess him I thought about how I would engage him in conversation. Drawing on my knowledge of the basic tenets of Islam as well as part of my childhood spent in Muslim majority northern Nigeria, on meeting him I was able to get beyond his initial hostility by simply saying, 'As-salamu alaykum.' This universal Islamic greeting spurred him to ask me, 'Are you Muslim?' Even though I shook my head, he was still intrigued enough to enable a conversation to ensue. With the help of his family I was able to get him admitted to hospital on the basis of a commitment to ensuring his religious beliefs would be respected.

The Wiccan

In the early noughties during a routine outpatient psychiatric evaluation in Brighton, a young local woman, on being asked about her spiritual and religious beliefs, looked me straight in the eye and said, 'I'm a Wiccan witch.' She then went on to regale me with the wide range of spells she had tried to cast over the years. I took as detailed an account of her musings as I thought necessary. However, what I had to keep in mind was the need to evaluate how much of her professed belief system affected her presenting symptoms of anxiety and depression. My respectful listening allowed her eventually to admit that part of why she had sought psychiatric help was fear of dabbling further with the occult. This admission allowed us to formulate jointly a support plan that included access to chaplaincy.

The guilty Christian

An evangelical Christian minister's wife presented to the outpatient clinic, depressed and facing the possible end of her marriage due to her infidelity. She had been on a course of antidepressants with limited lasting benefit. Having seen her a number of times, it became clear to me that she was struggling to reconcile her religious beliefs with what she had done. She was thus self-critical and feeling removed from her faith on account of her guilt. I decided to explore with her how she would go about addressing this 'crisis of faith' as a core component of her recovery from depression. Over the subsequent months her increased ability to reflect on how her faith could be a source of succour and relief helped her to address the issues in her marriage as well as improve her mood.

These should highlight a basic premise, which is that a tactful and respectful approach to the discussion of spirituality or religiosity within the context of psychiatric assessments is imperative. This holds true even if the belief systems revealed are at odds with the worldview of the mental health professional. Practitioner curiosity and open-mindedness are as important as the use of any particular framework. Indeed, patient spirituality should be approached as a treasure trove of understanding that increases the potential to impact positively on the patient's mental health and wellbeing.

Consequences: why bother?

It is important to remember that the spiritual dimensions of human existence become prominent, or sometimes even pre-eminent, at times of strife and adversity. Psychiatrists are a key component of the delivery of mental healthcare in the UK. As such, their ability to undertake a spiritual assessment with an acceptable level of proficiency is crucial. The use to which the information gathered from a spiritual assessment is put is dependent on the context and relevance to any agreed therapeutic objectives. On the other hand, if there are potentially harmful consequences of newly acquired spiritual practices, mitigating them through appropriate counselling and other spiritual rehabilitation might be necessary.

References

Anandarajah, G. and Hight, E. (2001) 'Spirituality and medical practice. Using the HOPE questions as a practical tool for spiritual assessment.' *American Family Physician* 63, 81–92.

Cook, C.C.H. (2004) 'Addiction and spirituality.' *Addiction* 99, 539–551.

Cook, C.C.H. (2013) *Recommendations for Psychiatrists on Spirituality and Religion.* Position Statement PS03/2013. London: Royal College of Psychiatrists.

Culliford, L. (2007) *Love, Healing and Happiness: Spiritual Wisdom for Secular Times.* Ropley: O Books.

Koenig, H.G. (2008) 'Concerns about measuring "spirituality" in research.' *The Journal of Nervous and Mental Disease* 1996, 5, 349–355.

Mental Health Foundation (2007) 'Making Space for Spirituality: How to support service users.' Available at https://www.mentalhealth.org.uk/sites/default/files/making_space.pdf, accessed on 31 May 2017.

Pulchaski, C. and Romer, A. (2000) 'Taking a spiritual history allows clinicians to understand patients more fully.' *Journal of Palliative Medicine* 3, 129–137.

RCPsych (Royal College of Psychiatrists) (2014) 'Spirituality and Mental Health.' Leaflet. London: RCPsych.

PART 2: THE BROKEN SPIRIT

Andy Nuttall

Andy Nuttall, DipHe, commenced nurse training in 1993 at the Berkshire College of Nursing in midwifery, qualifying in 1996 with a DipHE (mental health), and has since achieved modules in student mentorship and mental health risk assessment. In 2016 he qualified as a best interests assessor as part of the Deprivation of Liberty Safeguards. Andy has worked on inpatient wards in Slough, in Sydney, Australia, and in Brighton, and as a mental health liaison nurse in the A&E Department in Brighton. Andy is currently lead educator for mental health and mental capacity for Brighton and Sussex University Hospitals NHS Trust.

Healthcare setting

As a son of a vicar and of a teacher for young people with learning disabilities, I was perhaps destined, or doomed, to end up in the caring profession. I had very little interest in the human body at the time of my career choice of nursing, but much more interest in the human mind. I felt that people with mental illnesses and mental health problems got the least input, the most stigmas, and the most misunderstanding. I qualified in 1996 as a registered mental health nurse and have worked on inpatient units, in the UK and Australia, and spent the majority of my career working within a mental health liaison team in a busy city centre acute hospital. The team has responsibility for assessing patients presenting with a mental health problem through the Emergency Department, and to assess patients within the hospital with mental health problems. I also provide teaching to clinicians on mental health in general and on the Mental Capacity Act.

Definition and explanation of spiritual needs

The first instinct when defining spirituality and spiritual needs is to think of religion. I recall my first contact with spirituality in the 'Relating to religion or religious belief' definition of the English Oxford Living Dictionaries very vividly. I was a newly qualified mental health nurse in my mid-20s, in an inpatient unit in a multicultural area. I was (trying!) to care for a 6'2" Hindi lady who was definitely in a 'manic' phase of her illness. She was very excitable, and whilst attempting to ensure her symptoms did not cause too much risk to her or other patients, and no doubt trying to placate, she insisted I convert to Hinduism, and as she was happily and repeatedly striking my back so hard that the wind was being knocked out of me, I agreed. Foolishly, I wore an earring in the 1990s, which, in celebration of my conversion, she ripped out. (No harm done, the clasp released without drama.)

The English Oxford Living Dictionaries (2010) also defines spirituality as, 'Relating to or affecting the human spirit or soul as opposed to material or physical things'.

The Mental Health Foundation (2017), defining 'what is Spirituality', identifies the following factors:

> ...their religion or faith, meaning and direction in their life, sometimes described as their 'journey', a way of understanding the world and their place in the world, a belief in a higher being or a force greater than any individual, a core part of their identity and essential humanity, a feeling of belonging or connectedness, a quest for wholeness, hope or harmony, a sense that there is more to life than material things.

The Royal College of Nursing defines nursing as, 'The use of clinical judgement in the provision to enable people to improve, maintain, or recover health, to cope with health problems, and to achieve the best possible quality of life, whatever the disease or disability, until death' (RCN 2014, p.5).

I would argue that to nurse – to improve, maintain or recover our patient's mental health – the nurse would need to explore the 'wholeness' of the person, their 'identity'.

The Royal College of Psychiatrists (2014) offers a more general view, recognising not one clear definition, believing spirituality is:

...something everyone can experience, that it helps us to find meaning and purpose in the things we value, that it can bring hope and healing in times of suffering and loss and encourages us to seek the best relationship with ourselves, others and what lies beyond. These experiences are part of being human.

Motivation for asking about spiritual needs

My first 'contact' with the need to ask about spirituality came as student nurse when learning about models of nursing and specifically about Roper's 'Activities of Daily Living', which incorporates 'death and dying' and refers to spirituality. This section, part of 12 activities of daily living, was nearly always left blank, deemed to be somewhat 'taboo'.

In my more recent practical experience of assessing people presenting in an acute hospital with a mental health problem, my role generally involved completing a psycho-social assessment of a patient's needs, incorporating a risk assessment. The assessment would look at the whole person, their mental state, their physical health and their social circumstances – a holistic approach. To look for the whole person, an assessor needs to find out about someone's spirit, their identity, in order to establish what has gone awry, leading them to an A&E Department or to an act of self-harm or a suicide attempt.

Guidance on asking about people's spiritual needs

I often felt like I was assessing or supporting people with a 'broken spirit'. Many attendances to the Emergency Department were the first presentation to mental health services. I had the first opportunity to provide the listening ear. A theoretical approach I learned and adopted was the Rogerian belief of 'unconditional positive regard' (McLeod 2014). This is a 'basic acceptance and support of a person regardless of what the person says or does'. The need to offer acceptance of anyone's beliefs and values underpins an assessment.

When preparing to assess a patient with an exceptional presentation, such as a jump from a height with multiple injuries or a gunshot wound to the face that caused multiple neurological problems, or a lady who had given birth to a still-born child as well as having schizophrenia, I have realised I have taken my own spirit, or my own 'essential humanity', for granted. How do I prepare myself for a potentially distressing presentation, how do I convey the calmness obviously required to reassure the patient that they will be accepted, how do I convey an openness to reassure the patient that it is allowed to disclose their own story in their own words without being judged?

This could be argued as the identity of the clinician, the humanity, and the sense of connectedness with the patient. Without this, I do not believe I would be in a position to be able to understand the patient's own spirit, however broken or disjointed.

Despite the long-term effects of being involved in thousands of assessments of people with a vast array of mental health problems and potential 'burnout', I am reassured of my own ability to recall specific cases that have had a profound effect on me. I can distinctly recall an assessment of a patient who had jumped from a height, acquiring significant injuries. He had had minimal contact with services previously, and I felt privileged to be the one he told his 'story' to. It was the story of a broken spirit, of a broken man. One of the skills I learned as a student mental health nurse was the counselling skill of active listening. One component of this is to not think of what you are going to say next when listening to someone. This can be a challenge when assessing, as there are requirements for an assessment and, to some degree, an amount of ticking boxes. To actively listen to this patient, I believed my ability to connect through listening, not talking, was paramount to identifying where the problems lay leading to such a dramatic event. The Mental Health Foundation (2017) has also identified that their research highlights that 'developing one's own cultural or spiritual perspectives' aids recovery, and the ways that can be achieved is to 'be believed in, and of being listened to and understood'. I listened, I attempted to understand, I believed him, I believed in his ability to recover. I wanted to convey that. He described an adult life of failure, of repeating the same mistakes, both in his personal life and with his finances, and the hopelessness that resulted. He felt he couldn't tell his family, couldn't ask to be 'bailed out' again, and saw suicide as the only way out. The fact that he was willing to tell me was down to two factors, the first being the clinical necessity to be assessed, to give an account in the context of a history taking, but also, I believe, my ability to 'connect', to actively listen, to offer hope, and acceptance of his broken spirit.

Despite a multitude of broken bones, many weeks later he was able to walk out of hospital with the knowledge that he had been accepted by the team of nurses and doctors I worked with, but also by his family and significant others. I rarely crossed this line, but we hugged as he left. I knew very well that (hopefully!) I would never see him again. I felt his spirit had been gradually repaired, and he certainly gave me an enhanced sense of purpose to my role, and lifted my spirits, and still does.

To summarise a 'story' into professional guidance for asking about spiritual needs, I would focus on adopting a holistic approach, looking at the person, their spirit, what makes them tick. I would adopt a non-judgemental style, referring to 'unconditional positive regard' and openness, not just in your own mind and attitude, but also in your body posture. A presentation of external calm, whatever is going on internally, assists considerably to reassure people. I would always attempt to listen actively, however difficult it is to achieve, let alone master. This, I could interpret, is the spirit of the clinician, the humanity of the clinician, that I utilised. These skills will hopefully lead the healthcare professional to understand the patient's own identity, with the goal of assisting the patient on the road to recovery. I can recall simply, via a thorough assessment, establishing what the person would want to be doing with their life and simply asking, 'Right, what do you need to help you get there?'

Both the Mental Health Foundation (2017) and the Royal College of Psychiatrists (2014) provide guidance as to what could be considered spiritual activities, such as spending time with nature, playing music, taking part in sports or physical exercise, or doing voluntary work.

From my experience of working with people who are low in mood or have intense emotions, however tempting it may be to recommend such an activity for a person's spiritual wellbeing, there is a sense of 'if I could do any one of those things, I would'. Their experiences of mental health problems prevent them from just doing them. Small, achievable targets, which will slowly increase confidence, would be a better starting point, and demonstrates that the clinician has taken into account the patient's experiences.

My current role involves teaching around the Mental Capacity Act (2005), which has some interesting pointers within the legal framework of the Act towards exploring someone's spirituality, their identity, their wholeness. It is designed to protect anyone's rights to make their own decisions when they are deemed to have mental capacity to make specific decisions. It also ensures clinicians make decisions in someone's 'best interests' when that person is unable to make decisions for themselves. The Mental Capacity Act Code of Practice (2007) refers to the best interests 'checklist', which includes a statutory requirement that 'the person's past and present wishes and feelings, beliefs and values should be taken into account'. Spirituality, as defined by the Royal College of Psychiatrists, includes 'meaning and purpose in the things we value'. It is therefore reasonable to have a statutory requirement to pay due regard to someone's values, their spirituality, when making decisions on behalf of those who are unable to make decisions for themselves.

The Court of Protection, which oversees complex cases regarding mental capacity, made an interesting ruling in 2015 relating specifically to a patient's long-held beliefs. A mentally unwell man, deemed to lack capacity regarding a specific medical decision, was referred to the Court for a decision regarding his best interests. The judge spent a considerable amount of time with the man and gave the following statement, which, to me, links both English Oxford Living Dictionaries' definitions of spirituality referred to earlier:

His religious beliefs are deeply meaningful to him and do not deserve to be described as delusions: they are his faith and they are an intrinsic part of who he is. I would not define (Mr B) by reference to his mental illness or his religious beliefs. Rather, his core quality is his fierce independence.

The ruling encourages everyone involved in healthcare, whether physical or mental, whether the person is able to make their own decisions or not, to explore who our patients are. What makes them whole? What makes them connected? What is their humanity? What is their spirit? (Court of Protection 2015)

By using our own skills, our own humanity, we can make a difference, however insignificant it may feel at the time, to our interpretation of the patient's potential spiritual needs, on their own road to recovery, to repair their own broken spirit.

References

Court of Protection (2015) *Wye Valley NHS Trust v. Mr B*. Available at www.39essex.com/cop_cases/wye-valley-nhs-trust-v-mr-b, accessed on 2 February 2017.

English Oxford Living Dictionaries (2010) *Definition of Spirituality*. Available at https://en.oxforddictionaries.com/definition/spiritual, accessed on 2 February 2017.

McLeod, S.A. (2014) *Carl Rogers*. Simply Psychology. Available at www.simplypsychology.org/carl-rogers.html, accessed on 2 February 2017.

Mental Capacity Act Code of Practice (2007). London: The Stationery Office.

Mental Health Foundation (2017) *Spirituality* and *Recovery*. Available at www.mentalhealth.org.uk/a-to-z/s/spirituality and www.mentalhealth.org.uk/a-to-z/r/recovery, accessed on 2 February 2017.

RCN (Royal College of Nursing) (2014) *Defining Nursing*. London: RCN.

RCPsych (Royal College of Psychiatrists) (2014) *Spirituality and Mental Health*. London: RCPsych.

Roper-Logan-Tierney Model of Nursing: Based on Activities of Living. Available at www.nursing-theory.org/theories-and-models/roper-model-for-nursing-based-on-a-model-of-living.php, accessed on 12 February 2017.

4

Gynaecology

CARE FOR THE WHOLE

Peter Larsen-Disney

Peter Larsen-Disney, BSc (Hons), MBBS, FRANZCOG, FRCOG, FRCS (Edin), CGO, is Australian born but has been permanently resident in the UK for the last 16 years. His first degree was in science, and he was busying himself in a laboratory when he realised that he really wanted to work with people rather than rats. He completed his medical degree at the University of Melbourne and studied obstetrics and gynaecology at Monash Medical Centre in Melbourne. Peter then moved to the UK and spent three years working in obstetrics and gynaecology and in general surgery. He returned to Australia to complete his sub-specialty in gynaecological oncology, and settled momentarily into a consultant post in his old teaching hospital in Melbourne. In 2001, Peter returned to the UK to set up the Gynaecological Cancer Centre in Brighton, where he has worked ever since.

A human being is so much more than the sum of their physical components, and whether you are religious or not, I believe that all of us recognise this. There is a part of us all that makes us 'us', and whether we identify this as 'a soul' or just 'the spirit' of a person is somewhat irrelevant to my mind. It follows therefore that since a patient is a human being, they, too, must have a part that, for want of a better word, we shall call their 'spirit', and this may be based on a deep religious belief in one, a love for nature in another, and a passion for football in yet another. You disregard this part at your peril because it is only through recognising it that the whole patient can be seen and cared for.

But surely we are trained just to provide physical care to our patients? Well, yes and no. We do that, but if we are going to be better than just a machine applying algorithms appropriate for care, we must tailor care, taking into account the whole patient, including their spirit. It is easy to dismiss this as the remit of the chaplain, but the reality is that you and your team see a lot more of your patient than the chaplain can. I would argue therefore that you must hold yourself responsible for the administration of holistic care, including a push for physical and spiritual wellbeing.

We have all seen the effects of spiritual distress brought on by a patient's situation: anxiety, psychosomatic symptoms, unrealistic expectations, agitation, fear, depression, unresolved anger or guilt, and so on. I believe that the only way that the clinician can assist with this is if they establish a rapport with the patient and this requires trust. I also believe that trust can only be forthcoming when the clinician dedicates time to it. We are all time-depleted as we rush from one clinical commitment to the next, but the trick is to make the time we have count.

I often hear myself telling my junior doctors 'not to treat the blood pressure, but rather to treat the patient'. As I explain to them, if the patient is well and the blood pressure isn't at a worrying level, then it just doesn't need treating. In a similar way, I always emphasise that it is important to treat the patient, and not the disease. Let me illustrate with three examples.

Jemma was 25 years old and a mother of two. She had an aggressive tumour that had recurred rapidly after surgery and adjuvant treatment, and unfortunately, it was clear that she would not survive for more than a couple of years at best. Jemma, unsurprisingly, found this totally unacceptable.

Mavis was 92 years old, riddled with arthritis and had major issues with her mobility. She was teetering on the brink of needing to leave her home that she had lived in for over 60 years and move into a nursing home. We had now discovered the slow growing tumour in her belly, and if she didn't die from something else, this was likely to slowly progress over a couple of years. She wasn't fit for surgery and the prospect of a couple of years of gradual decline was not something she relished the thought of. In fact, she made it clear to me that she would happily accept euthanasia.

Gertrude was also 92 years old and presented after falling off a ladder whilst cleaning out her gutters. She, too, had a tumour and at best guess about two years to live (unless something else caught up with her), and was very angry. 'Doctor', she said to me, 'I have responsibilities, I have a 93-year-old husband to look after, and I need to be around.'

The message is clear: just as a disease must be seen in the context of the individual person, the individual must also be seen in the context of their social situation. It is a wise clinician who seeks to know the patient sufficiently well in order to gain an understanding of the relevance of the disease to the individual.

Thirty years ago, as a medical student, I was told again and again not to become too involved with my patients, as this was seen as inappropriate and, I guess, a threat to the objectivity required of the dispassionate clinician.

One day, a senior clinician walked into a small tutorial group I was attending with tears in his eyes and he said, 'All of your medical career you have been told not to get involved with your patients, and I tell you that's bullshit! How can you really care for your patient if you don't get involved?'

This was a 'eureka moment' for me because I felt that I was given permission to do what I felt instinctively to be right. Why not get involved? Not to the point where you would 'take on the disease yourself', but rather to the point where you could share the pain a bit, empathise, comfort and give the patient the opportunity to share their fears or concerns, enabling you to understand what the disease meant to them, and thus how best to help them with their situation. I think much of this is about being a good listener. It is not about probing, but rather about giving permission for the patient to share their feelings and to explain the significance of their response to their situation. It is a great compliment to be taken into a confidence, and I often say that it is a privilege to help someone at the time of their worst imagined crisis. That is one of the most rewarding aspects of my job.

To be successful in allowing someone to open up about their situation, it may be necessary to share some personal information, but only to the point where you remain comfortable. Such open sharing in my experience often helps with trust without in anyway jeopardising the professional relationship required. It is also of critical importance not to impose your own views on matters outside your professional remit. It is perfectly within the rules to share personal information you are happy to share but it is not, in my view, appropriate to share details of your own belief, either secular or religious, but rather to reflect back, where appropriate, the patient's beliefs freely expressed to you.

Communication and finding out what makes patients tick

When I was a junior registrar, a senior consultant once said to me that a patient will trust and believe in you if you give them your undivided attention for even a few seconds, and momentarily make them feel like the centre of your universe. They must be the foremost thing in your mind for that period of time, however fleeting that may be. That time allows you to build a personal relationship that fuels trust.

A clinician should never lie to a patient; you must deliver truth or the patient will see straight through you. Good communication and relevant information will often defuse the somewhat daunting pace of change that is associated with severe illness and deteriorating clinical condition. Patients are often grieving the loss of their good health when you see them, and whether they can be cured or not is irrelevant. Calm understanding and clarity of information will often provide spiritual succour to the patient and their family.

Often a patient will give you a clue about what is important to them. They may volunteer that the local parishioners are praying for them or they may bless you, which is a pretty good indicator of an underlying religious belief. Others may surround themselves with pictures of their family and it takes little to get them to talk about their children and grandchildren. I often find an open question like, 'What do you do when you are not stuck here in hospital?' results in an insight into their personal interests or spirit, and remembering this and using it in a future line of enquiry is invaluable.

Adapting to 'the spirit' is important. Rather than 'we plan to discharge you on Saturday', we could 'aim to get you home in time for the big match' or in time to 'have some bubbles at your grandson's birthday'. It is personal and recognises what is important to that person.

A simple question like, 'What are you thinking?' may give you all you need in order to know how best to help someone and to understand what their 'spirit' needs at that moment. It goes without saying that such intimate disclosures must be respectfully handled, and privacy should be the best you can offer on a busy ward.

Is it okay to have fun?

Carol had a really nasty sarcoma with a really nasty prognosis. She found it very difficult to talk about this with her husband who was fairly lacking in emotional maturity, and was determined to grit her teeth and pretend 'this just isn't happening'. She opened up a bit to the nursing staff but really couldn't communicate her fears to anyone. I saw Carol getting herself more and more wound up and depressed. One day I decided to do a ward round armed with a voice-activated dancing weed. I stopped at the end of the bed and demonstrated to Carol the fine art of making the weed dance. Carol's face that hitherto had looked like a blank mask showed a flicker of interest, and then I asked her to see if she could make the weed dance. Somewhat to my surprise, Carol grabbed the weed and screamed expletives at it, and we were rewarded with a rapidly gyrating weed. One thing led to another and the ward round was abandoned as all the patients and staff ended up in fits of laughter. Carol completely changed after that. She had dissipated her frustration and anger at her diagnosis and become much more real in her approach to her situation.

I remember seeing my boss shaking his head after he had witnessed 'the voice-activated dancing weed incident'. He asked me what I thought I was doing. I replied that Carol needed a good laugh and I had given her that by getting her to dispel her frustration by screaming at the weed. 'Will we ever change you?' he asked. 'I certainly hope not, sir,' I replied.

I use humour a lot. There are very few people on this earth who don't like a bit of humour, but the argument against using it with patients is (in my experience) that if you joke with a patient, they won't know when you are being serious. I am yet to see a patient in whom this is true. The very same patient who laughs with you will listen intently when you need to have a serious chat about problems or a poor prognosis. In fact, they are likely to do so because you have treated them as you would wish to be treated – as a human being. I have derived such pleasure over the years by joking with my patients and seeing their faces light up despite the nasty situation in which they find themselves.

Liz had a really unpleasant vulval cancer, and she knew that she would need pretty major surgery to remove it. Of course, this has real implications for a woman and the potential for psychosexual problems afterwards is considerable. Liz was sexually active and was really very upset at the thought of losing her clitoris and we talked about this a lot before her operation. Patients never fail to surprise me with their resilience, but Liz went further than most. She turned a really sad and personal thing into a very public one and held a huge 'wake for her clitoris', inviting everyone she could think of to the party, and then passing around a hat for donations. I should add that this raised hundreds of pounds for cancer research, and she came in for surgery the next day full of mirthful stories of the party, and I honestly believe that this allowed her to cope so much better than she would have otherwise.

I am not sure that there is scientific evidence to support this, but my experience is that a happy patient definitely does better than a sad one. A happy patient is usually motivated, and this sees off the risks of complications because they are up and about and fighting to regain normality. We have all had patients who steadfastly refuse to budge from the bed or refuse to 'push' themselves, and it is really important to understand the spirit of these people as it may allow you to identify the trigger you need to motivate them. Sometimes just understanding what is holding them back is enough. A little spiritual sustenance can work wonders.

Everyone is different and flexibility is important

It is easy in our game to fall into a regimented pattern. For example, with the introduction of the enhanced recovery programme, patients are expected to be home on day four post-op, even after a major laparotomy. We work towards this target, but it is really important to be flexible. The patient who is emotionally struggling with their situation may need extra time or indeed may need early release from hospital. I can think of two recent patients, both of whom had done brilliantly post-op.

Fatima revealed that she was terrified that her husband would reject her because she would not be able to fulfil the expectations of her cultural background once she got home. She was brave enough to share this and we were able to address it with appropriate input from her husband and her imam. She went home confident and secure a few days later than the usual.

Vera was fiercely independent, and became increasingly irritated by other patients whom she blamed for disturbing her sleep at night and distracting her during the day. She eventually told us how much she was missing her cat (who apparently was her closest and probably her only friend) who calmed her by sleeping on her lap and on the end of her bed. Her delight at being allowed to escape on day three was a joy to behold.

Follow-up of patients after their operation has historically been the norm. In the not too distant past, all patients subjected to the surgeon's blade would be reviewed at six weeks to check that they had recovered from the surgical assault administered and to screen for complications. Increasingly, we don't routinely follow up our patients, but it is really important to recognise that some patients will need that contact in order to be confident into the future, even if their post-op consultation is nothing more than a quick chat and a check of the wound. It is my experience that many patients who have had a chronic course pre-operatively will need closer follow-up, and even if the surgery has cured their problem, you may need to manage 'the whole' with a couple of reviews that occasionally may even be ongoing while the patients recover their confidence and ultimately their independence. Other patients will be very satisfied with 'discharge' on the day of their surgery providing you take the time to discuss the operative details fully, and make sure that the patient is happy with any post-op instructions.

Cancer patients have historically always been seen post-op for regular follow-up appointments. It is written on 'stone tablets' that they should be seen three-monthly in the first year, four-monthly in the second year, six-monthly in the third year and then annually in years four and five. At that point they are deemed cured and discharged. I have a few problems with this approach. First, there is no evidence base to support it, and second, it seems illogical to treat a good prognosis tumour the same as a poor prognosis tumour. Given that we are all reminded regularly to practice evidence-based medicine, my doubts about this blanket approach led me to ask the question: if there is no evidence to support routine follow-up of cancer patients, would my patients want it? My guess was that 50 per cent would want the reassurance of regular review by their consultant and the other 50 per cent would not want to put their children into child care and take two buses into the hospital just to see me if it wasn't necessary and of proven benefit. I put this to the test and surveyed my patients. I was slightly upset to find out that 90 per cent of my patients didn't want to see me if it wasn't necessary. There are lessons to be learned here. We don't really know what our patients want unless we ask them. So again, it is important to be flexible and to take the time to find out what is important to any given patient.

Janet was seen six weeks after a laparoscopic hysterectomy for endometrial cancer. Her cancer was low grade and on final pathology very early. I guess her surgery gave her about a 95 per cent chance of long-term cure. I offered her the option of patient-initiated follow-up – no regular reviews, but immediate access if any symptoms developed suggestive of recurrent disease. Janet was thrilled because she wanted to put the cancer behind her and get on with her life. At many levels it would have been wrong to drag her back for regular review, especially as her chances of cure were so high.

Gloria was seen six weeks after a laparotomy for early stage ovarian cancer. Her chances of cure were probably about 80 per cent, but she was still convinced that it was inevitable that the cancer would return and 'see her off'. She was a dependent soul and someone who had considerable faith in me (I should add that it took me six weeks and several consultations to convince her to let me remove the mass in her belly that made her look like she was carrying a full-term pregnancy). To suggest that Gloria could have functioned without regular review and reassurance would be madness. She needed regular review, and I saw her for her regular follow-ups and sometimes on other occasions simply to allay her fears.

Rosie had had chemotherapy, followed by major surgery and then further chemotherapy to treat advanced ovarian cancer. She was a very stoical lady but volunteered to me at one point that she didn't sleep for the week before her follow-up consultation, because she was fearful that I would discover a recurrence when I reviewed her in clinic. She also went off her food and developed diarrhoea that lasted for the week up to her appointment, and then after her review she returned to normal. To date, Rosie's tumour has not recurred, but it will, and she knows it. Everyone is different, and we must be prepared to individualise our care to optimise the quality of life of any given patient. In Rosie's case, we agreed not to monitor her with tumour markers that could tell us if the tumour is recurring six to nine months before it becomes clinically apparent, as she had become fixated with meaningless fluctuations in levels. We also gave her some counselling to help with her fear of review in the hospital, as it became clear that these visits reawakened the horror she had felt when her 'healthy life had been snatched away by the doctor who told her she had cancer'.

Thorny issues in obstetrics and gynaecology

Ethics is never that far away from us in medicine, but I think that obstetrics and gynaecology has more than its fair share of ethical dilemmas to deal with. As with so many things, context is everything, and it is really important to understand the context rather than just the clinical scenario. Again, I would emphasise it is important to treat the whole patient and not just the illness. The only way this can be achieved is to listen carefully and ask sensitive questions to establish the situation. Failure to do so can lead to some very awkward situations, so I would suggest that this sort of history taking is both helpful and a good investment of time.

Beth was 43 years old and had married late after a very successful career in the rag trade. She and her husband had tried for three years to achieve a pregnancy, and with 'the biological clock ticking' they finally resorted to IVF. Beth had two unsuccessful cycles of IVF, but finally became pregnant with the third cycle. She had an early ultrasound scan that confirmed a viable intra-uterine pregnancy but then presented at ten weeks gestation with bleeding and pain. Beth and her husband Mark were devastated when the pregnancy miscarried.

Barbara was 45 years old and had three children in their 20s and late teens. She was convinced that she was perimenopausal and was confident that she didn't need to worry about contraception. She was wrong! Having convinced herself that her lack of periods were due to her climacteric, she only discovered that she was pregnant when she presented as an emergency to A&E. Barbara's relief was palpable when she miscarried at ten weeks gestation.

Brianna was 18 years old when she presented with pain and bleeding in pregnancy. She was unsure of the dad's identity, and despite the promise of help from her parents who were keen for her to keep the pregnancy on religious grounds, she had decided to have a termination. She was booked for this the following week, but Mother Nature intervened and Brianna lost the pregnancy at nine-and-a-half weeks. She was very happy with this course of events and promised to be more careful about contraception in the future.

Each of these three patients had the same clinical condition, but it is obvious that the significance of the condition was vastly different for the three women involved. Ipso facto, the discussions undertaken at the bedside were, by necessity, very different.

The modern era allows us to spot problems in pregnancy in a way that wasn't possible even a generation ago. Many parents now opt to screen their baby for problems, and one common example of screening is the test for Down's syndrome. Applied early and with ever increasing accuracy, parents can know whether the baby is affected with this (and several other genetic disorders). In addition, it is usual to have admired your baby many months before it is born thanks to the ultrasound probe, but this generally happy invention can reveal many a problem.

Jo and Peter had two healthy children, and given that they were sliding into the 'elderly parents' group at school, they wanted to have a screening to see if their new baby was 'normal'. They were extensively counselled and had already decided that if their baby had Down's, they would want to keep it, but wanted to be prepared for the eventuality. Jo's screening blood test led on to an amniocentesis, and Down's syndrome was confirmed in their little boy. Subsequent scans showed no major anatomical abnormalities, and Jo went on to deliver a healthy baby boy who was gratefully received by them and their children.

Lisa was 37 years old, and was found to have a Down's syndrome baby when she had screening in her early pregnancy. Lisa was devastated and without hesitation insisted on a termination as she could not cope with the thought of having 'a retarded baby'.

Jane had an early ultrasound that confirmed her own fears that something was wrong with her baby. The scan showed multiple abnormalities that were incompatible with anything other than a few days of life. Jane was a devout catholic and wouldn't consider termination of her pregnancy. She had a normal delivery of an obviously abnormal baby girl and showed nothing but joy when she held her infant, oblivious to her problems. Jane nursed her little girl until she died a day and a half later. Her devotion and bravery touched many of our staff.

It takes sensitivity and patience to deal with each of these situations, and it is essential that you don't fall into the trap of applying your own moral stance, but rather, you have to manage the whole situation by applying your understanding of the 'whole person' involved. Taking the time to 'know' the patient means that you can administer the care that that individual requires. It is so important not to judge but rather to support, whether the patient's beliefs align with your own or not.

Gynaecological oncology can throw up some very challenging situations. I have been deeply affected by many of these, and it is important to understand that to be affected is okay.

Clare was a mother of four who presented at 16 weeks pregnant with bleeding, and was found to have a large cervical cancer. Delaying treatment was going to result in further growth of her cancer and would certainly increase her risk of death due to the cancer. Clare was deeply religious and found herself in a horrible situation. We talked at length about options, and ultimately Clare justified immediate surgery to remove her tumour (and her pregnancy) on the basis that it made it much more likely that she would be around to look after her other children. She spent a lot of time with the unborn baby she had lost, and spoke openly with her children about the loss of their little brother.

This case highlights the need to help patients reach their own decision in a time of crisis. I felt deeply honoured to be involved in discussions about Clare's deepest beliefs and how to work through this awful problem. She ended up, after much supported personal reflection, in a situation where she knew what was right for her and her family, and I had made it clear that I would respect her decision and support her no matter what that decision was. She remained well after treatment and has often updated me on the successes of her three daughters and her son.

Beth was 31 years old when she was told she had ovarian cancer. Her treatment required the loss of her uterus and ovaries, and the potential impact of this was profound. Beth would be rendered menopausal at only 31, and would also be rendered infertile. Beth had no children and desperately wanted them, and therefore she asked whether she could freeze some eggs to use in a surrogate pregnancy.

I explained that the better option was to freeze embryos rather than eggs, but this begged the question about whether Jake, her boyfriend, would step up to the mark and father her children. To add to the complexity of the situation, I had to discuss with Beth the fact that her cancer was likely to have a genetic basis and had to ask the question, 'Do you want to risk freezing your eggs or embryos in the knowledge that you may well pass on the genetic disorder to your children and potentially give them cancer?' I also had to go to that dark question, 'Do you really want to produce children in the knowledge that you may well not be around to see them grow?' This is really tough stuff to deal with, and once again the key is to provide the facts and guide the patient and their partner through the ethical issues to a place that they are comfortable with. Your own thoughts must be kept locked away if you are going to be able to provide them with objective information that will inform their decisions.

Jenny was 46 years old and the mother of three children aged 11, 9 and 5. She was dying of disseminated malignancy and chose to be admitted to our ward during her last few weeks of life, as she wanted to die in a place she knew well and with nursing staff and doctors she had known for years. She felt safe on our ward, and wanted to do this bit away from her husband and family. They visited her often and had really good quality time, but when they left, Jenny swung into action and planned their future. She had numerous checklists that she worked through to make sure that everything was in place, and even went so far as to interview a series of nannies to choose the right one for her kids. Jenny spent lots of time with her three children individually, and prepared them so well for her death that they stood up and gave the eulogy at her funeral. I tell you there wasn't a dry eye in the house when those kids spoke about their mum.

Occasionally our patients choose to die on our wards, and this is one of the greatest compliments we can be given. For a patient to trust you enough to allow you to care for them during their final days is a privilege. To be honest, our dying patients are treated the same way as our living ones, and I know that our team shows the same respect to all, but with the dying patient it is more important than ever to treat the whole person, to understand their spirit and to ensure its comfort in just the same way as we provide their physical care.

The majority of our patients are cured, but still we have plenty with life-threatening or terminal diseases. Our patients seldom complain about little things because they are too busy dealing with the big issues. I think that they must be the most grateful patient group on the planet because they elevate you to an unjustifiable status if you cure them, and even if you don't, they are so grateful that you joined them on the journey and tried to do your best.

What is a good day?

A good day in my book is the one in which you make a difference. I remember once getting home late one night and my wife asked me, 'How was your day?' I replied that I had had a really good day. Intuitively she asked, 'What does that mean, did you do a good operation or did you have a good death?' I can't remember which it was, but both are equally important.

Most of my days are good ones. Despite the usual hassles of not-enough-time, not-enough-beds, not-enough-resources, the good days still keep coming. I guess when the good days cease to come, I shall have to stop doing this job, but until then I shall continue to love my job and hope I will always find the time to listen to the 'whole' patient and be amazed by the way they cope with what life throws at them.

5

Neonatal Care

Cathy Garland

Dr Cathy Garland, MB, ChB, MRCPCH, is a consultant neonatologist at the Trevor Mann Baby Unit in Brighton, where she has worked for the past seven years.

> *If of thy mortal goods thou art bereft*
> *And from thy slender store two loaves alone to thee are left*
> *Sell one, and with the dole*
> *Buy hyacinths to feed the soul.*
> (Saadi Shirazi)

Introduction

Having a sick baby in the Neonatal Intensive Care Unit (NICU) can be a very traumatic time for the family.

He is ventilated and unstable, and the monitor alarm keeps ringing off. He has lots of lines and tubes. You can't cuddle him, because he's too unwell. The staff keep using lots of words and abbreviations that you don't understand. He may die. If he survives he may have long-term learning difficulties or cerebral palsy.

You may also be two hours from home. Your baby was moved here because he was too ill for the local unit, or he needed surgery. You have two other young children at home, and you're trying to sort someone to look after them.

Maybe you're 14, and this wasn't planned. The staff keep asking you to express milk, because it's the best thing for your baby's tummy.

Or perhaps you're 40, and this is your fifth round of IVF. He's your last chance to be a mum.

This isn't what they talked about at antenatal class. This isn't what you wrote on your birth plan.

The above are all actual situations faced by our families.

Or you could be the baby in the incubator. You have lots of tubes and lines for the ventilator and another in your nose for getting air out of your stomach. Every four hours someone sticks a needle in your heel to take a blood gas sample. And the doctors are on their fourth attempt to site a cannula in your hand. It hurts. The alarms are really noisy, and the lights are very bright. Just when you're comfortable someone turns you over again to examine you or change your nappy.

There are a number of weighty texts discussing neonatal *physical* care and, for the purposes of this chapter, suffice it to say that as doctors and nurses looking after these tiny and vulnerable patients, we must always strive to provide the standard of care that we would want for our own baby. This requires knowledge, skills and especially attitude – a commitment to provide the best possible management for each baby, a willingness to seek help or advice and an ability to acknowledge our mistakes and to learn from them. A good neonatal nurse or doctor doesn't have to know everything, but we do have to be passionate about finding solutions to what matters for our patients.

My aim in this chapter is to describe how we endeavour to care for the *spiritual* needs of our babies and their families.

Spiritual *adj.* 1. relating to the spirit or soul and not to physical nature or matter. (*Collins English Dictionary* 1998)

The older I become, and the more experience I have as a doctor, the more I realise how important it is to treat and care for the whole patient, and their family, mind, body and soul. I have no claims to expert knowledge, skills or insight in this area. This chapter is more a reflection on things I have learned through my work, and also my personal experiences. I hope that you enjoy reading it.

The baby's rights, and our aims

As soon as a baby is born, he has full individual rights as per the United Nations (UN) Convention on the Rights of the Child (1990):

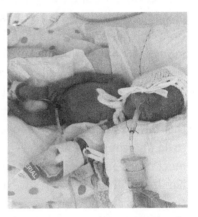

> ...the best interests of the child shall be a primary consideration...

> ...ensure the child such protection and care as is necessary for his or her wellbeing, taking into account the rights and duties of his or her parents...

Dolly, twin 1: 23 weeks
gestation, birth weight 486g

Additionally, the General Medical Council (GMC) *0–18 Years: Guidance for All Doctors* (2007) states:

> Doctors must safeguard and protect the health and wellbeing of children and young people. Wellbeing includes treating children and young people as *individuals* and *respecting* their views, as well as considering their physical and *emotional welfare*.

> When treating children and young people, doctors must also consider parents and others close to them; but their patient must be the doctor's first concern.

It's heartening to see that guidance from both the UN and the GMC alludes to the whole child, not just the child's physical needs, and also emphasises the importance of considering parents.

Spiritual care of the baby

PAIN, POSITIONING AND COMFORT CARE

None of us likes pain. When babies are ventilated, cooled for neuro-protection, post-surgical or having painful procedures such as lines or blood tests, we should keep them comfortable. Strategies for this range from boluses or continuous infusions of morphine or midazolam, to more basic but significantly effective solutions such as offering oral sucrose, a dummy, swaddling or containment holding.

Whilst in their incubators our babies are 'nested' to offer them comfort and security. We have incubator covers to stop the unit lights shining in their faces, and place a cover over their eyes when using a bright light to do procedures. Noise levels are monitored, and there are scheduled quiet times on the unit, when lights are dimmed, and there is minimal handling. Similarly, babies wear mini ear muffs when going through the MRI scanner, which is very noisy. For the older babies, we place developmental toys or musical mobiles in their cot to give them some interest and stimulation, and if parents are not present, the nurses take them out for cuddles. Pain, discomfort and over-stimulation by light or noise are stressful: we should use the 'what would I want in their shoes?' approach.

PRIVACY AND CONFIDENTIALITY

> Children and young people are individuals with rights that should be respected. (GMC 2007)

It's always fascinating how we would not stare at or openly talk about an adult patient in a hospital bed, or being wheeled down a corridor, yet it seems acceptable to do this to a neonate. I know that this is frequently because people are just interested and feel sympathy, but as a neonatal team, we strongly believe that an infant's privacy and confidentiality should be respected in the same way as that of an adult.

On the neonatal unit, parents and visitors are requested not to look at or discuss other babies. When performing procedures, we place a screen around the cot space, and we place a cover over the neonatal transport incubator when moving a baby around hospital corridors.

For infant and parental privacy and confidentiality reasons, we have a policy that we only pass on information to a baby's parents. Likewise, written information pertaining to a neonate should be treated and respected in the same manner as that of an adult patient and according to Caldicott guidance (DH 1997).

PARENTAL LOVE

> Love is patient, love is kind...it is not self-seeking... It always protects, always hopes, always trusts, always perseveres. (St Paul AD 55)

The normal carers and comforters for a baby are his parents. Even when their baby is on a ventilator, parents are encouraged to touch him, do 'containment holding', change nappies, and become fully involved with his care. The ITU (Intensive Treatment Unit) can be a frightening place, and it's lovely to see parents' confidence increase on a daily basis.

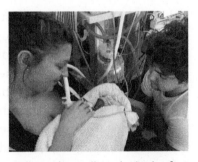

Dolly, on the ventilator, having her first cuddle with parents Shona and Darren

As soon as is safely possible, babies are taken out of the incubator and placed on mum or dad's chest for kangaroo care, cuddles and initiation of breast-feeding.

Parents are allowed to visit at any time 24/7, and can stay during procedures if they wish. For logistical reasons such as space and noise, we have visiting times for other friends and relatives.

The love and bonds that form between an infant and his parents over the first two years are essential for his emotional development, and his future interactions and relationships with others. It is essential that we provide a supportive environment for the initiation and development of this bonding.

The spiritual needs of parents

As indicated by the stories at the beginning of this chapter, huge burdens are placed on the parents of our patients. I believe that as a neonatal team, we have a responsibility to consider and care for their spiritual and physical needs, as well as those of our babies.

COMMUNICATION

> Nature hath given men one tongue but two ears, that we may hear from others twice as much as we speak. (Epictetus AD 50–135)

I think that the mainstay of achieving this is to develop a caring and professional relationship, with open and honest communication. This spans from the first point of contact, which is frequently antenatal, throughout the duration that the baby is under our care.

Doctors of my generation had little, if any, formal teaching on communication, and either learned by observation of seniors, or from our own mistakes and successes. My interest in this area started a number of years ago when I read a series of articles by John Diamond, a journalist who was diagnosed with throat cancer, and eventually died. He wrote about his experience, and made some salient observations about communication by health professionals (Diamond 1998).

Following some further reading around this subject, I started to run 'Breaking Bad News' sessions for juniors, with a long-suffering nurse wearing my dressing gown and cuddling my daughter's baby doll. They were interesting and formative sessions for all of us.

Happily, times have changed, and communication skills are now taught throughout medical school and junior doctors' training. Parental communication is a very important part of the Resuscitation Council UK Newborn Life Support (NLS) and Advanced Resuscitation of the Newborn Infant (ARNI) courses that we run for medical and nursing staff, and also of our regular in-house and Deanery neonatal simulation sessions.

I think that some basic points to remember are:

- Be completely honest and truthful: parents will then trust you.
- Show you care.
- Speak slowly and use language that parents will understand.
- Avoid abbreviations and jargon.
- Listen to what parents are saying, and their concerns.
- Allow plenty of time.
- Don't be afraid to say 'I don't know'.
- Remember only a small percentage of communication is the actual words spoken: the way in which those words are conveyed, eye contact and body language account for a much greater part.
- Don't overload parents with information.
- Ask if they have any questions, and try to answer them honestly and clearly.
- Offer to meet again to go over things.
- Don't take away all hope. Even if a baby is going to die, there is the hope that the family can spend some special time together, and have some good memories, and that the baby will be with them and comforted.

When a mother is admitted in preterm labour, a senior member of staff goes to speak with both parents on the labour ward. As well as describing the practicalities of what will happen at the time of delivery, we counsel regarding the issues of prematurity, according to this infant's gestation. Where appropriate, we discuss the possibility of death and long-term disability including cerebral palsy, learning difficulties and problems with hearing and vision.

Similarly, for antenatally diagnosed abnormalities, we meet with parents in the antenatal clinic. We explain about the condition, its management and likely outcomes. We invite parents to visit the unit. Newcomers to NICU often find it an odd and scary place with lots of machines and alarms. Parents have a chance to see this, and start preparing and making adjustments in their own minds.

In the cases of very extreme prems such as 23 and 24 weekers, I say, 'It may be that your baby is not alive at birth, or is in such a poor condition that it is not in his best interests to resuscitate him. If this happens we will give you your baby to cuddle. We will be there to support you.'

Similarly, 'When we do get your baby up to the unit it's a case of taking things a day at a time at the beginning. Your baby may develop problems with his lungs, or become so unwell that it is not right for him that we continue intensive care. We will be honest with you about these things.'

On NICU, parents are constantly updated at the cot side, by the nurse and doctors caring for their baby. They can be present during ward rounds and medical handovers, which they find reassuring as they feel they are fully involved and informed. Their opinions are valued.

As a medical student and junior doctor, I thought that consultants had to know everything about their specialty and have all the answers. I now realise this is not the case, and am happy to be open and honest about this. I say that I will discuss their baby with colleagues at the grand round, or seek a specialist opinion. Interestingly, in my experience, parents have found this reassuring. Rather than being frightened by our lack of some specialist knowledge, they are comforted by our determination to do our best for their baby, including our willingness to be open and to learn.

Sometimes we need to tell parents bad news. This may be that their baby has had a significant deterioration, or a new concerning diagnosis. It is essential to get this right, as parents will re-live this moment for the rest of their lives. In this situation, I meet with parents in a private room, with the baby's nurse, a box of tissues and a 'Do not disturb' sign on the door. Plenty of time needs to be set aside.

It is so important to be honest with parents, and involve them in decision-making. Ultimately, they will be the baby's support for the next 18 years and more. My involvement with this new person is for the duration of their NICU stay, and then a few outpatient visits. Theirs is 24/7 and lifelong.

PARENTAL CARE AND ACCESS

The physical contact and bonding described earlier is important for the emotional and spiritual wellbeing of parents, as well as of babies.

Sometimes parents have a feeling of helplessness. They feel as though everything is out of their control. By comforting their baby and being involved with their care, some of these anxieties are alleviated.

After delivery and resuscitation, we show parents their baby on the Resuscitaire® and let them touch

Albert, twin 2: 23 weeks, birth weight 617g, having 'kangaroo care'

him and take photographs, before taking him to NICU. Similarly, when we are retrieving a sick or premature infant out of a local neonatal unit, once the baby is stable in the transport incubator, we take him to his parents on the labour ward, before going to the ambulance. We discuss his current clinical care, and expected course, and ensure they have the phone number of the receiving NICU. We check when mum will be moved to join her baby and try to expedite this.

PARENTS IN THE AMBULANCE

In 2010 we introduced a policy of allowing a parent to travel with us in the ambulance. Initially, this was just for repatriation of stable infants back to local units, but now we also allow a parent to travel in the ambulance on emergency journeys. Families really appreciate this opportunity, and our transport team quickly embraced the change. It's what we would want if we were a parent in that situation.

'It was nice just to be with him.'

'That I could be with her the whole time and know that she was okay.'

'Everything was explained and I felt very supported.'

'Every mother should be allowed to stay with their baby.'

We presented this data as a poster at the UK Annual Neonatal Transport Interest Group Conference to encourage other teams to do the same. The Department of Health *Toolkit for High Quality Neonatal Services* (2009) and the Bliss baby charter (2015) both advocate allowing parents to be with their baby whenever possible.

Sussex Neonatal Transport Team loading the transport incubator into our neonatal ambulance

RONALD MCDONALD
AND PARENT FACILITIES

Neonatal intensive care is a specialised service and many of our families are a long way from home. For these parents, we provide rooms in our 'Ronald McDonald' accommodation, a charity run by the fast food chain. Parents have somewhere free to stay, where they can go to sleep and eat, yet still be very near their baby. Some parents end up staying in these rooms for weeks. They are such a bonus for families, but sadly are not available in all NICUs.

On the unit itself we have a parents' lounge with toys, a kitchen with free tea, coffee and milk, and toilet and shower facilities. There are also three rooms where parents 'room-in' with their baby. These facilities are so important for parents. Families often spend large amounts of time apart, which has a significant toll on relationships with partners and other children. Mums have said to me that they feel so torn between their baby in intensive care and their toddler who says, 'Mummy, you don't love me anymore,' because they are away from home so much. This parents' area provides a space where other children can play, relatives can wait during visiting times, and parents can relax and chat. They get to know other parents on the unit and share experiences. We are very grateful to our supporting charities Rockinghorse and the Early Birth Association, for financing these facilities.

GOING HOME

For the short-stay babies this is just a happy and natural progression. Parents are grateful for our care, but glad to be going home. For other families, this is the final stage in a long journey. These babies have been on the unit for weeks or months. Their parents have come to know and trust us. They have built up their confidence to some extent, but the thought of having their baby at home alone with them is very frightening.

We are fortunate to have a neonatal outreach team who get to know the families in special care, help plan and facilitate discharge, and then visit the family at home. Nearing the time of discharge, parents spend even more time on the unit, learning how to do 'cares', and how to give medication. They are taught basic newborn resuscitation. Some parents even learn how to do nasogastric feeds, change colostomy bags and perform rectal washouts.

Monitoring is gradually weaned down, and when their baby is ready for home, his parents 'room-in' for one or two nights. They have their baby with them in an en suite room next to the unit and undertake all his feeds and cares, with 24/7 back-up just down the corridor. When their baby is eventually discharged home, families know that a familiar face will call round the next day to help sort any issues, and they find this very reassuring. They can also phone the outreach team or the neonatal unit for advice over those first few days.

After discharge home, we follow up many of the infants in outpatient clinics. Parents also frequently bring their babies back to the unit to see us, and send in photos and cards. Many become involved with our fundraising charities, or organise their own fundraising events, anything from sponsored sporting exploits to raves on the beach! We also have a regular parents forum that a consultant colleague and matron attend.

For infants who have come to us from other areas, we repatriate them as soon as it is clinically possible, so that the family can be nearer to home. This is sometimes a really difficult move for parents. They have become used to one team, one place and one way of doing things. During my neonatal transport work, on a number of occasions parents have become upset, and tearful even, because everything seems so different. One example is that a number of other units have a policy that repatriated infants should be placed in a side room until surface swabs have come back negative. Parents are afraid that their baby is on his own, and that something could happen and no one would notice. Equally, parents repatriating to our unit sometimes find it difficult.

One of the challenges in caring for parents is to understand that what seems routine to us can often be very anxiety-provoking for them. We have a responsibility to explain to parents that things will be different, to reassure them, and to be very positive about the receiving unit and team.

Death and dying

When he heard I was writing a book chapter, a friend said to me, 'Why don't you start it with "Once upon a time" and end it with "And they all lived happily ever after". That's how all good stories go.'

Sadly, real life isn't like that. For most people, the concept of their child dying is an unspeakable tragedy, worse than dying yourself. For some families, this is a reality they have to face during their time on NICU.

Some of these infants will die suddenly and unexpectedly. Some of them may have only been born a few hours before and been critical since birth. Others are a few weeks into their stay on NICU, and then have an acute deterioration. One minute they are relatively stable, and then within a few hours, despite full intensive care and attempted resuscitation, they are dead.

These sudden deaths are overwhelming, devastating, a complete shock for parents. Their hopes are suddenly shattered. Their lives will never be the same. When this happens on NICU, we do our absolute utmost to have both parents present and to make this situation as bearable as possible. We explain to the parents that we are doing everything we can, but not succeeding, and that their baby is going to die. Or that although we are giving full intensive care at the moment, we know future prospects are so grave for their baby that it is not fair, and not in their best interests, to keep doing this.

If there is time, we ask if they would like their baby to have any religious ceremony and arrange for this to happen on NICU. We explain that we will not let their baby suffer but will keep him comfortable with painkillers and sedation. We also explain that sometimes babies can make some gasping movements, but that these are reflex responses and that their baby is not in pain.

We offer parents the choice to hold their baby in their arms during those final minutes and ask if they want this to happen in NICU, with screens around and no other parents in the room, or if they would prefer to be in the parents' room on the unit. If the latter, we quickly arrange the practicalities. The baby has one allocated nurse who will be with the family for the rest of her shift. If possible, we let the parents have some time to cuddle their baby whilst he is still on the ventilator. We turn off the monitor so that all the alarms do not go off, and so that parents do not watch the heart rate and saturations on the screen. They can take photographs together, and other family can be present. Doctors generally leave the family with their nurse so that this is a personal and private time.

When the parents are ready, or if we feel the baby is slipping away anyway, the ETT (breathing tube) is removed, and again, we leave the family together with their nurse. The nurse will then come to collect us when the baby has died, so that we can certify death. There is no rush for this to happen, and I much prefer it if they are absolutely sure the baby is dead. Babies' heart rates can keep going very slowly for many minutes. If the baby still has a heart rate, I just say to parents that he hasn't quite gone yet, but he is nearly there and is very comfortable.

When a baby is dying, we have a duty to him to ensure that he is pain-free and comfortable. We use morphine for the former, and midazolam for the latter. I have friends who have spoken of family members who have suffered during those final hours or minutes, and I think that this is an unnecessary tragedy. I give my patients enough medication to ensure they are completely settled, and in no pain or distress.

After the baby has died, his nurse then helps his parents to bath or dress him. They can take hand and footprints and more photographs. They are given a memory box, where many parents place the baby's cot card, ventilator hat and other items that remind them of their baby's short life, and which help them come to terms with their grief.

Parents can have as much time as they wish with their baby, in the parents' room, and with other family present. If parents so wish, they can take their baby home for a few days. We have to ensure that the police are informed, and they need to keep the body cool. Another alternative is to take their dead baby to the children's hospice where they have a special room with a bed that has a cool mattress. Families can spend time together there, with play areas for siblings, and meal facilities. Parents can take their baby out in the beautiful garden in a pram.

Most families choose to leave their baby in the hospital, and the nurses take him to the mortuary dressed and snuggled in a Moses basket. After a baby's death, his nurse contacts the family's GP and health visitor, so that they can offer further support when the family are at home. It also hopefully prevents professionals who do not realise the baby has died contacting the family with inappropriate questions or information. This can be very distressing for parents.

Families are given information about registering the baby's death and making funeral arrangements. If the baby has been on the neonatal unit for a long time, families often really appreciate it if members of staff attend the funeral. Families are also given contact details for the various bereavement charities. Unfortunately, we do not at present have a bereavement counsellor on our unit. We know this is an omission, and one of our sisters is presently training for this role. This will be a real bonus as she will have a true insight into the family's time on NICU, as well as counselling skills.

It is mandatory to discuss all our infant deaths with the coroner, who will occasionally request a post mortem (PM). Generally, a PM is not obligatory, but it may frequently reveal information that was not previously known, and which may be useful to the family, either to help them come to terms with this death or for future pregnancies. We offer a PM to all families. Many decline, because they feel as though their baby has been through enough, or because they want to have an early burial for religious reasons. Unless a coroner's PM is needed, we respect the parents' wishes. Organ donation is another option in some circumstances. Again, this is a complex area, but for some families it can offer something positive from the tragic loss of their baby.

Approximately six weeks after an infant's death we offer a follow-up appointment for the family, either in an office on the unit, or in another building if they prefer. Most families take up this offer and find it a useful step in the grieving process.

Taking babies home to die

My brother died in a climbing accident when he was 22. This was obviously sudden and unexpected. His body was brought home and placed in the front room with the curtains closed, for family and friends to come and pay their respects. My family wanted it that way. My grandfather died at home when I was 21. He didn't want to go into hospital, so with the GP's agreement, family cared for him at home, with visits from the district nurse. I was with him when he breathed his final breaths and it was very peaceful. He stayed there till the funeral.

I would like to die at home, in my bed with my three dogs and plenty of morphine to keep me pain-free, and midazolam to make me relaxed. Similarly, some of our families have strong feelings about how they would like things to be at this difficult time. Sadly, 99 percent of babies who die still do so on a neonatal unit:

For many the opportunity of consistent support through this time, to take their baby home or to consider the use of hospice services, is not available as it is for older children. This needs to change. (Andy Cole, Chief Executive, Bliss, quoted in McNamara-Goodger 2009)

On our unit we are trying to make this change for our families. We openly discuss parents' wishes and hopes and do our best to fulfil them.

Some infants have life-limiting conditions but do not require intensive care support. Examples include infants with inoperable congenital heart disease, trisomy 13 or 18 or congenital osteogenesis imperfecta. From the time of diagnosis we are completely open with parents, explaining that their baby will die. We say that we want the time they have to be a special time for them all. Parents are understandably devastated by the diagnosis that may not have been made antenatally.

Over the next few days or weeks, we try and involve parents as much as possible with their baby's care and build up their confidence, and a relationship of trust. From the beginning, we introduce the idea of taking their baby home to die, with ongoing support. We speak with their GP, and introduce the family to the paediatric community nurse team and a named paediatrician. That way, if the family find they are not managing, they can be admitted seamlessly to the children's hospital. We also discuss the alternative option of going to the children's hospice, as described above.

It is essential to have a frank discussion with the family about the infant's Do Not Actively Resuscitate (DNAR) policy, and they sign a written agreement. As well as the above professionals, the Emergency Department and ambulance services need to be made aware of these babies, so that inappropriate resuscitation is not undertaken.

For some families, taking their baby home is really important because they have other children to look after. Any time at hospital means time away from them. First-time parents may feel they want to take him home to have time as a family, away from the stress and busyness of the unit.

Three of our families kindly agreed to share their stories and photographs in this chapter, with the hope that this will help other health professionals realise the possibilities of taking babies home for end-of-life care, even for babies on the ventilator. I am very grateful to Ralph, Evelyn and Katie's parents for this, and for everything that they have taught me.

Ralph had trisomy 18, and after a period in hospital, his parents, Gemma and Grant, took Ralph home for comfort care. He was their first baby. After his death, at 63 days, Ralph's parents wrote me a beautiful letter describing how:

> We indeed did make precious memories, spending time with family, friends and most importantly just the three of us... We continued to give our son all the love, care and devotion possible knowing that was all we could do for him yet realising that was enough and all he really needed... Since Ralph's passing we feel a great sense of sadness and emptiness that I can't begin to describe. We know as a couple we have to find a positive route for our future and learn from Ralph's strength and determination. Giving in to sadness and despair would only be an insult to his precious life... A conventional funeral didn't seem right for Ralph, us, or our loving families. So we had Ralph's ashes made into fireworks we named 'Ralphies' Rockets'. Each with their own personal tribute on from his adoring family. We sent them up into the sky along with a promise we would hold him in our arms again some day!

Some infants with life-limiting conditions are on full intensive care. At parental request, we have also taken these infants home, or to the hospice, beach or a local beauty spot for withdrawal of intensive care. Other parents have asked to take their baby home on the ventilator for a few hours and then return to the unit for extubation.

In these situations, we transfer the baby in the neonatal transport

Ralph at home with his father, Grant

incubator, in our ambulance, with a senior doctor and nurse. We take a pram, portable ventilator and gases, so that parents can push their baby around the garden, or seafront, and have time together. We ensure that the baby has adequate comfort care (morphine and midazolam), and feed or fluids. When the family are ready, we remove the breathing tube, and let the family be together.

These journeys take time and also a willingness to work outside of the box. I advise parents that some difficulties may arise, and we discuss contingency plans. I strongly feel that the benefits for families far outweigh any potential difficulties.

Evelyn had non-ketotic hyperglycinaemia, and was ventilator-dependent. We took Evelyn and her parents, Kathryn and Craig, in the ambulance to a local beauty spot that was a special place for them, for end-of-life care. Evelyn had time with her parents feeding the ducks and having cuddles. We took Evelyn off the ventilator, under the trees by the lakeside. Evelyn died that night at Chestnut Tree House Hospice. Evelyn now has a little sister, Maisie.

| Evelyn having cuddles | Evelyn with her mother Kathryn, at the lake |

We would be more than happy to share photos from when we were at Swanbourne Lake if these are going to help convince other teams how very special this service is to parents... Our time at Swanbourne Lake and then at Chestnut Tree House was extremely precious to us.

We are forever grateful that we had that opportunity and didn't have to say our goodbyes at the hospital. (Kathryn and Craig)

Katie was born at 32 weeks and had hypoxic ischaemic encephalopathy. She was ventilator-dependent. At her parents', Helen and Steve's, request, we took Katie home for the day, where she spent time with her parents and the family cat in the garden, having cuddles, eating lunch and opening Katie's presents. It was a beautiful sunny day. Katie died that night on the neonatal unit, in her parents' arms, and with some flowers from home. Katie now has a little brother Toby.

Katie having cuddles

Katie at home in the garden, with her parents, Steve and Helen

Myself and Helen would be more than happy to send you some of the photos we took as a family the day we came home. We look at them every day as we had a number of them framed and put up around the house. Thank you once again for all the team's support and for allowing us our day at home... It was such a wonderful opportunity for which we will be forever grateful. (Steve and Helen)

I never fail to be amazed by the love and resilience of many families. The human spirit is strong.

The personal toll

A problem shared is a problem halved.

On bad days I think I would like to be a sheep farmer on the Yorkshire moors. My job is very interesting, incredibly rewarding, but also at times exhausting, stressful and emotionally draining. For me, my sources of strength and comfort are my colleagues at work, my family and friends (including canine) at home, and my personal faith.

As a neonatal team it is vital to support each other, to have the ability to walk into a colleague's office and discuss worries about a patient, or offload about a bad night. Sometimes it is the listening ear that helps, sometimes the chocolate biscuits and humour. Senior doctors support junior doctors. They also need to support each other. Within the confines of the office, or clinical meetings, we are often are very frank and honest with each other about infants on the unit. We need to share the heavy burden of clinical responsibility in the very challenging patients, such as redirection to comfort care.

Doctors are bad at taking time off sick, and at sharing their personal woes. It is therefore important to look out for each other. I have been on both the advising and the receiving end of conversations to go home and have some time to recover, or spend time with a sick family member. As in every other walk of life (including sheep farmers), doctors and nurses suffer from anxiety and depression, have counselling, and take medication to try to overcome these.

> Depression is at least as common in the medical profession as in the general population, affecting an estimated 12% of males and up to 19.5% of females.
>
> However, because of the stigma associated with depression in almost all cultures, which seems to be greatly magnified among medical practitioners, self-reporting likely underestimates the prevalence of the disease in medical populations.
>
> Indeed, although physicians seem to have generally heeded their own advice about avoiding smoking and other common risk factors for early mortality, they are decidedly reluctant to address depression,

a significant cause of morbidity and mortality that disproportionately affects them.

Of all occupations and professions, the medical profession consistently hovers near the top of occupations with the highest risk of death by suicide... (Andrew 2016)

Just as this book is about considering the emotional and psychological needs of patients and families, I think that as health professionals, and as a society, it would be good to change our attitude to illnesses of the mind and spirit. People readily talk about cancer, surgery or other physical illnesses, and yet we shy away from acknowledging mental illness or emotional problems. I think times are changing.

On our unit we now have a staff counsellor two days per month, funded by one of our charities. Any member of staff on the unit can attend, and colleagues will cover their hour away. This not only makes sense morally, but also financially, by supporting and strengthening our workforce.

I am also incredibly grateful for support from family and friends at home. It is highly advisable to cultivate another life, outside medicine.

Enlightenment

For family reasons, I recently spent a significant amount of time visiting the Neurology Intensive Care Unit in Leeds. The words at the opening of this chapter were scribed in an ornate pattern on the floor outside the lift lobby. Like the flowers in the beautiful garden and the light coming through the stained glass windows in the chapel, they lifted my spirit. We can find beauty and joy in our surroundings. It can also come from the kindness and compassion of the doctors and nurses who care for us, and our families.

References

Andrew, L.B. (2016) *Physician Suicide*. Available at http://emedicine.medscape.com/article/806779-overview, accessed on 1 February 2017.

Bliss (2015) *Family Friendly Accreditation Scheme: Helping to Make Family-Centred Care a Reality on Your Neonatal Unit*. Available at www.bliss.org.uk, accessed on 1 February 2017.

Collins English Dictionary (1998) Millennium Edition. Glasgow: HarperCollins.

DH (Department of Health) (1997) *Report on the Review of Patient-Identifiable Information*. The Caldicott Committee. Available at http://webarchive.nationalarchives.gov.uk, accessed on 1 February 2017.

DH (2009) *Toolkit for High Quality Neonatal Services*. Available at http://webarchive.nationalarchives.gov.uk, accessed on 1 February 2017.

Diamond, J. (1998) *C: Because Cowards Get Cancer Too*. London: Vermillion.

Epictetus, Greek philosopher (1909–14) *The Golden Sayings of Epictetus*. New York: The Harvard Classics.

GMC (General Medical Council) (2007) *0–18 Years: Guidance for All Doctors*. Available at www.gmc-uk.org/guidance/ethical_guidance/children_guidance_index.asp, accessed on 1 February 2017.

McNamara-Goodger, K. (2009) *A Neonatal Pathway for Babies with Palliative Care Needs*. Bristol: Association for Children's Palliative Care. Available at www.togetherforshortlives.org.uk, accessed on 5 April 2017.

Saadi Shirazi, Persian poet, 13th century. Available at https://en.wikipedia.org/wiki/Saadi_Shirazi, accessed on 1 February 2017.

UN (United Nations) (1990) *Convention on the Rights of the Child*. Available at www.unicef.org.uk, accessed on 1 February 2017.

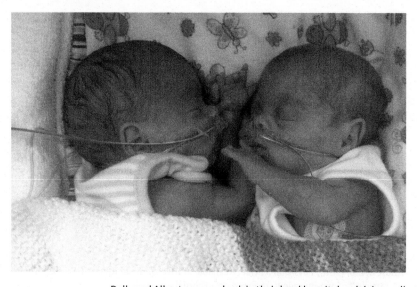

Dolly and Albert are now back in their local hospital and doing well

6

Paediatrics

THE UNFINISHED CONSULTATION

Somnath Mukhopadhyay

Professor Somnath Mukhopadhyay, MBBS, DCH, FRCPCH, MD, PhD, is Chair of Paediatrics at the Royal Alexandra Children's Hospital and the Brighton and Sussex Medical School. He graduated from the University of Calcutta (now Kolkata), India in 1983. He has worked in the NHS in England, Scotland and Wales for over 32 years. Professor Mukhopadhyay is the academic lead for paediatric research and teaching within the Brighton and Sussex Medical School, and works closely with colleagues at the Brighton and Sussex University Hospitals NHS Trust, aiming to develop innovative approaches for healthcare in children. His clinical and research interests lie in the fields of children's allergy and asthma. His research and public engagement work is helping to develop a growing interest in personalised medical approaches for common childhood conditions such as asthma and allergy.

Daisy is a six-year-old with severe eczema, allergy and asthma. We have been following Daisy up for several years now, and her symptoms are proving very difficult to control. Daisy attends with mum who is an organised person and usually enters with a list of questions in her hand. The asthma has twice gone out of control in recent months. The nights are a little bit less sleepless but still pretty unbearable from the constant itching. Daisy has multiple allergies. We have already withdrawn milk and egg from her diet; are we now going to withdraw wheat too? Is it time to consider one of the immunosuppressant medicines that mum and dad understandably have many concerns about? The next two patients are already waiting. There is just about time to complete the physical examination, explain any changes in therapy and write out the odd urgent prescription. It is now time to say goodbye to Daisy and her mum.

As Daisy walks out of the consulting room, a quiet child with red, dry, scaly skin, tired face that speaks of sleepless nights, clinging to mum's trousers, uncertain steps, a frail goodbye, I wonder as I write my notes what else there might have been to talk about.

Is Daisy an anxious child? If so, for how long has she been anxious? What might worry her? Have the young parents been in conflict and if so, could that have had a negative impact on Daisy's mind? Has Daisy's chronically red and inflamed skin made her a victim of name-calling and other little games at school, when one child is often isolated for the benefit of more general entertainment? When Daisy is sleepless at night, what are her thoughts? How might this thinking interplay with her immune system? Do they make her skin more inflamed and itchy? Do they then tighten her little chest and make her search for her reliever under the pillow, or call out for her mum and dad, in the middle of the night? Are these external circumstances, primarily related to family and society, influencing the course of Daisy's illness?

Is the worry and anxiety settling in Daisy's mind largely influenced by external circumstances, such as her interactions with her carers or her friends, or is this worry and anxiety principally a reflection of how Daisy's own mind *reacts* to such external circumstances? Some human beings, including children, could be more vulnerable to such external 'trauma' while others could be more resilient. Thus, some children and adults could be closer to a quieter internal 'still-point' and this closeness could protect them from the disturbing effects of these external influences, while others may be much further away from this 'still-point' and thus could be more easily buffeted by such influences. A popular – and perhaps somewhat simplistic – way of defining this spread of individuals is by referring to people as being 'more mindful' or 'less mindful'. Recent work even attempts to measure this closeness to the 'still-point' as a 'mindfulness score' (Brown *et al.* 2011). Improving this state of mindfulness, for example, through mindfulness-based cognitive therapy, can improve psychological states such as depression and anxiety. Is it perhaps possible that the route to improving Daisy's condition lies not through giving her more and more steroids, or other medicines that have side-effects, but through improving her state of 'mindfulness' through prayer or related mindfulness-based practice, so that she is able to understand the ways her mind is reacting to these external influences? Would this allow her still pliable mind to correct itself and would the resulting increase in peace and serenity have a beneficial effect on the immunological cascade that is driving her eczema, asthma and allergy?

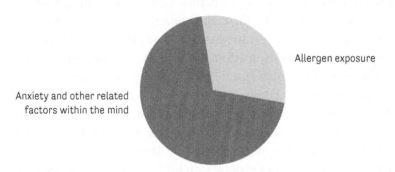

Allergen exposure

Anxiety and other related factors within the mind

Every child is different: possible causes of Daisy's illness

Medicine treatment for asthma is managed as 'steps'. The doctor starts off at step one, where the child is prescribed the 'reliever' inhaler alone. If 'reliever' need is high, or the child's asthma appears otherwise poorly controlled, the doctor will often prescribe regular 'controller' medicines, such as inhaled steroids. Further evidence of poor control could lead to the addition of increasing 'layers' of 'add-on controller' medicines.

Jamie, the next child on our outpatient list, is seven. His asthma remains inadequately controlled on a relatively high dose of regular inhaled steroids, the first-line controller medicine. He is taking his inhalers properly. The diagnosis of asthma appears to be correct – his chest tightness improves with his 'reliever' medicine, implying that an important reason for his chest problem is airway spasm that is relieved immediately by airway dilatation with 'reliever' medicine. This, by definition, is asthma. Within the short 10- to 15-minute time frame of a follow-up consultation in hospital or general practice, it seems appropriate to add on a further layer of medicine and this will, in many instances, provide better control of Jamie's symptoms. Of course, quite often it might not, and Jamie could go up the medicine spiral over time, and perhaps also continue to suffer from his symptoms.

There are, however, other important aspects to Jamie's history, if we have the opportunity and the intent to explore. Jamie's house is fully carpeted and his bedroom is stacked with soft toys that have historically belonged to his younger sister Gemma. Carpets and cuddly toys are breeding grounds for house dust mites, whose miniscule poo particles, invisible to the naked eye, can sensitise some children in whom they can then progress to worsen asthma and allergic disease. Gemma, now seven, has thwarted mum's repeated attempts to get rid of her toys. Also, there are two cats and a dog within the household, and although Jamie does not have any problems when he plays with the dog, he invariably starts sneezing when he is cuddling the cats. The asthma gets really bad during the summer months. Typically, Jamie starts coughing and spluttering when he is out playing with his friends on the small grassy patch overlooked by their block of flats during a warm spring or hot summer afternoon. This summer, the coughing and spluttering did not improve on one afternoon with his usual 'reliever' medicine. The coughing spasms got worse, Jamie found himself getting breathless, and he was very anxious because he started to feel he might not be able to draw in enough air with each breath to keep himself alive. There is perhaps nothing that provokes more anxiety in our minds than not being able to breathe in the air that sustains our lives moment by moment. His parents were also very worried and contacted the ambulance service that arrived promptly, administered oxygen and nebuliser medicine, and took Jamie to the Children's Emergency Department at the hospital that evening. He recovered in hospital over a week and missed school for nearly a fortnight.

What might be happening in Jamie's airways? If Jamie is sensitised to the dust mite and cat allergens, his airway tubes could be getting chronically inflamed through regular exposure to these allergens. This inflammation may not be enough to cause major asthma attacks, but it could be preparing the ground for other allergens such as pollen, or infectious agents such as respiratory viruses, to act on the already inflamed airways, leading to a full-blown asthma attack. As a result, Jamie could be developing asthma attacks when he is playing outdoors in the summer months, or picking up a virus infection in the autumn. By enquiring in greater depth about the personal story of his illness, we can often pick up leads that can be further supported by specific allergy testing. This may open up new options for Jamie and his parents and new lines of treatment for his doctor. A thorough cleaning of his room, the substitution of laminated flooring for carpets and re-housing the cats might improve his airways over time. If allergic inflammation is an important cause of Jamie's illness, anti-allergy medicines could work to reduce his dependence on inhaled steroids and reduce the need for more asthma medication.

Jamie is unique, and so is every other child with asthma and allergy, and indeed with any other disease. Ten-year-old Maya, who comes in next, also has severe asthma, but careful questioning does not identify any underlying triggers, as we had found for Jamie. However, Maya belongs to a group of children with airway molecules built in a way that leads to progressive worsening of asthma over time. Individual genetic codes for each child with asthma create the child's unique set of airway molecules. Maya has an 'adverse' genetic code that causes her airway molecules to secrete more inflammation-related molecules, which result in her asthma being worse than Jamie's, even without the influence of any external allergens. There is little scope for removing environmental triggers to alleviate her illness. Instead, we have to give her a higher dose of inhaled steroids, to suppress the inflammation of her airways, and this will improve her symptom control. She is different from Jamie.

Some allergens could be entering Jamie's body through tiny gaps in his skin. He has poor skin barrier function. This condition affects a tenth of children. These children have a gene change that makes it easier for allergens, such as cat dander and peanut allergen, to enter their bodies, trigger the process of sensitisation and create the ground for the development of allergy and asthma symptoms. Maya, on the other hand, has a firm skin barrier. The allergens entering through her skin are not worsening her asthma. Instead, Maya has a set of roguish airway molecules that are programmed to create a more inflamed environment in her airways, thus causing worse asthma. A careful allergy-focused history underpinned by appropriate allergy testing may allow us to control Jamie's asthma by reducing allergen exposure, while in Maya's case it could be more reasonable to try to contain these rogue airway molecules through more robust anti-inflammatory treatment, such as a higher dose of inhaled steroids, that aims to maintain good airway health and reduce the progress of the changes of long-term inflammation, such as the proliferation of fibrous tissue. Every child is different.

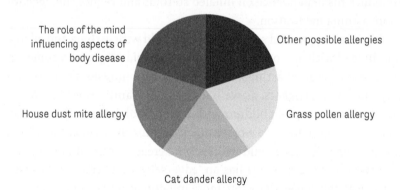

The role of the mind influencing aspects of body disease

Other possible allergies

House dust mite allergy

Grass pollen allergy

Cat dander allergy

Every child is different: possible causes of Jamie's illness. Some of the allergens could be entering through his weak skin

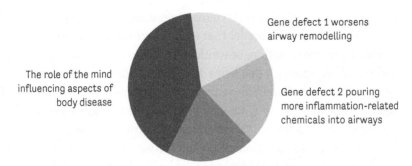

Gene defect 1 worsens airway remodelling

The role of the mind influencing aspects of body disease

Gene defect 2 pouring more inflammation-related chemicals into airways

Gene defect 3 increasing vulnerability to some external allergens but we do not know which ones

Every child is different: possible causes of Maya's illness

It is important to carry through our consultations so that we can differentiate between the Jamies, the Mayas and the Daisys, and help each of their families with the right advice, while recognising that the advice for Jamie is different from that for Maya or Daisy, and develop treatment plans that maximally benefit each child in question. Each well-rounded consultation could open up one or two avenues that are unique for the child and point towards interventions that will help the individual child in question. The avenues will differ from child to child. Our existing model of medical practice is more influenced by pharmaceuticals; we aim to control symptoms primarily through the use of medicines. This model is often effective. A large enough dose of inhaled steroids or steroid creams will often control the child's symptoms of asthma or eczema. It is also often the easiest treatment to put in place, from the healthcare point of view. The doctor usually requires less time to decide regarding increasing the dose of medication, or adding an additional medication, than to investigate the build-up of factors that could be leading to worse manifestations of disease in an individual. The 'one-size-fits-all' approach that relies more on the use of medicines is often more cost-effective and intrinsically easier to administer than the 'one-size-fits-one' approach that relies on creating a more individual body and mind profile for each child.

There are, however, several counter-questions. First, do patients and their carers prefer the model that relies more on medicines with less enquiry and investigation, or would they prefer doctors to take a more individualised approach that helps develop individualised disease profiles for the Daisys, the Jamies and the Mayas? My experience is that a lot of parents would like their children to be on as little medication as possible. As the doctor reaches for the prescription form, informed parents are often bristling with questions. 'How long do we need to maintain Johnny on these medicines?' (Answer: as long as he continues to have symptoms, and this could mean for many years.) 'What are the side-effects of this increase in dose or of introducing this new medicine?' (Answer: a large number of patients have been using the common asthma medicines for many years, and follow-up studies have not in general identified major side-effects with the use of standard doses. This is an important reason underlying our reliance on the 'pharmaceutical model', and this is helping patients enjoy a relatively good quality of life for many years. However, every medicine can have side-effects, and some additional side-effects of currently used medicines might be identified at a later date.)

Let us also consider what happens to our bodies when we administer some of these common medicines. It is perhaps difficult to imagine the lining of our lungs on which the inhaled steroids settle, as we cannot readily visualise the inside of our lungs. Instead, let us imagine a more visible part of our body such as our skin. The skin is the outer lining of our body. Asthma and allergy cause a kind of long-term soreness (inflammation that results in redness, swelling, irritation and other related symptoms) of the lung lining that often responds to 'anti-inflammatory' medicines such as steroids. A similar sore, with redness and swelling, can happen on the skin. Almost all of us will have experienced a sore on our skin at some stage of our lives. Steroids contain the inflammation. If we regularly apply steroids to this sore, there is a good chance the sore will get better. However, if there is an underlying cause for the soreness and the redness, the sore will not heal fully with steroid creams until we have removed this underlying cause. Imagine, for example, that you are wearing a bangle that contains nickel and this is causing a sore on your wrist because you are reacting to the nickel.

You have a choice: you can either continue to wear the bangle and also use a steroid cream for years to keep the sore under control, or you can stop wearing your nickel bangle, avoid wearing other nickel bangles, use the steroid cream for a few days to get rid of the sore and gain freedom from the problem. Which one of these two treatment choices appeals more to you? Let us now transpose this example to the lung, with at least one proviso – the situation in the lung is likely to involve not just one factor, as for the skin, but a number of different factors.

Thus, one way of managing asthma and allergy could be to explore as carefully as possible the factors that could be worsening asthma, to establish their causality through appropriate tests, and then to seek to remove these factors as far as practicable, while using inhaled steroids and other medicines only as much as is required to maintain satisfactory asthma and allergy control. It is possible that this approach may result in lesser use of medicines for symptom control, as the child might require lesser doses of controller medicine when some of the factors that could be making their asthma worse have been identified and removed. This approach will need to be more individualised. We know how Daisy, Jamie and Maya's illnesses are different, as a result of genetic and other influences, and we can seek to eliminate the factors worsening their individual illnesses only after we have properly identified them in each case. This approach will require additional time, and may also require additional training for some doctors and nurses. The other approach could represent perhaps not being as meticulous in exploring the external and internal factors that could be contributing to worse asthma, but using adequate (possibly larger) doses of controller medicines, such as inhaled steroids, to gain good control of symptoms. Which one of these approaches would you prefer?

This story of 'every child is different' could have an additional, relatively unexplored angle that is of relevance to the child and carer: is my child's medicine working to help my child or am I giving him a regular dose of chemicals that are relatively ineffective? A new medicine is considered suitable for clinical use if trials on many hundreds, sometimes thousands, of patients show the medicine to be more effective when compared to the currently used treatment or when compared to ineffectual treatment, such as with sugar pills, often referred to as placebo. However, when researchers look at only those children receiving the new medicine, without looking at the ones on placebo, they often find that, within this group, children respond to the new medicine to different degrees, with some children in this group perhaps showing relatively little improvement or no improvement at all. The response to a medicine could depend, for example, on the genetic code of the individual, and tiny differences in the gene code between individuals could mean that one child, or adult, will respond to the new medicine while another child will not. However, on entering clinical use, medicines are often not restricted for use in children with particular gene codes. They are prescribed for the entire population at a particular stage of the disease. It follows that a proportion of children may not respond appropriately to the medicine that has been prescribed, and this is true in asthma as in many other diseases. When a doctor prescribes a cholesterol-lowering medicine such as a statin, a blood test in a few months' time will show whether or not the medicine is working. Clinical improvements in asthma are often not as clearly defined. There are also a number of different aspects to good asthma control: for example, a child who has normal lung function at the clinic could still be experiencing symptoms at night or during exercise.

Katie is a 15-year-old referred to the doctor because the school nurse is concerned about her frequent school absences and her deteriorating performance at school. She stays in her room on Facebook during evenings, and wakes up at least a couple of times each night when her chest tightens, seeking relief from several puffs of her 'reliever' medicine. When she first attended the clinic a year ago, Katie admitted to the asthma nurse that she was taking her controller less than half the time.

Asthma nurse: 'There are seven days in a week and you are supposed to take your purple medicine twice every day. This comes to fourteen doses every week.'

Katie looks away from the nurse. 'Yes,' she says.

Asthma nurse: 'So, if you are being honest, how many doses of the purple inhaler do you think you take every week?'

Katie and her mother look at each other. Often this process could take time, but some children do eventually come up with an answer.

Katie: 'Five?'

Asthma nurse: 'This is why you are suffering every day from your asthma. How do you think you can better remember to take your purple inhaler more regularly? Would it help if you kept the inhaler beside your toothbrush, so that you are reminded to take the medicine day and night?'

This battle to improve adherence is sometimes a long and difficult one that progresses over many years, with the doctor, nurse and carer often on the losing side. We blame their teenage status and their 'hormones' for their rebellion against conventional medicine, and this could, of course, be part of the overall picture. However, I think we often do not give these young people the 'space' to tell us *why* they are not taking their medicine. If we think they are not taking their medicine, as in Katie's case, we try to persuade them to take their medicines more regularly. The assumption we make, as doctors and nurses, is that the medicine will make their asthma better and they need to understand this 'simple fact'. More often than not, we meet this silent yet powerful resistance. Our message often does not seem to have the desired impact. Medical interventions to improve adherence to therapy in teenagers with asthma have been generally poorly effective.

I have often wondered during these interactions whether the child is trying to tell us something through this silent yet powerful resistance. We got our first clue through our own studies that showed that controller medicines might not actually work in a proportion of children with asthma. This was supported by other work done by research groups in the Netherlands and the US. The controller medicine worked brilliantly in many children. In others carrying a particular gene change, one of the medicines in the purple inhaler worked less well, possibly because the gene change created an airway molecule that was different, and the medicine was interacting in a different manner to this protein, thus rendering it less effective in the child. What if Katie wasn't taking her medicine because she felt it didn't really make a difference to her asthma control? How good are we at creating the right environment in our clinics to let the Katies of the world tell us *why* they are not taking their medicines? Could Katie be different from other teenage children of her age in that she is reacting differently to her controller medicine? Could we expect Katie to take her medicine if she did not feel the medicine was making a noticeable difference to her asthma control?

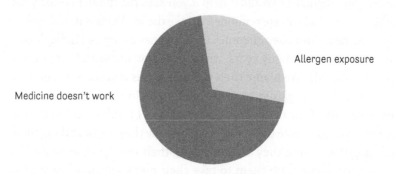

Every child is different: possible causes of Katie's illness

Asthma, allergy and eczema touch the lives of hundreds of millions of people all over the world. Written for the general audience, the purpose of this article is to encourage debate regarding which of the above two broad treatment approaches patients, carers, nurses and doctors might favour. We do not know if one approach is, on the whole, more expensive than the other. Thus, while 'finishing' our consultations could increase the demands on health professionals' time in the clinic, the process could lead to lower overall medicine costs in the long term, and the improved management could perhaps result in lower costs from reduced hospital admissions and reduced emergency visits to hospital Accident and Emergency (A&E) Departments and general practice. It could result in greater patient satisfaction and carer satisfaction. Crucially, the end result must be good asthma control, as good asthma control results in a better quality of life and reduces the risk of life-threatening asthma attacks. A more personalised approach to management must thus ensure good asthma control before any reduction in medicine treatment can be contemplated.

The unfinished consultation therefore has both soul and body aspects within the areas of consultation we have been unable to finish. Our aspiration for a holistic model is not just about integrating psychological aspects with existing, more physically orientated, dimensions of care as relevant for every child. It is also about ensuring that we deliver the physical dimension of care to an optimal level, individualised for each child attending the clinic. The typical consultation for a child with asthma and allergy is short, and it does not often explore the total illness. It is important to reflect on how we can strive to 'finish' our consultations for the children we manage. As healthcare professionals, in both hospital and general practice, we need to develop a deeper and more complete understanding of how physical disease interacts with the mind, and how we can help children overcome any unfavourable interactions that could be worsening their disease. Perhaps even more important, we need to think of how we can help future generations of trainee medical and other healthcare professionals move away from the existing pharmaceutical model of medicine towards a more holistic, yet personalised, model that seeks to address the unique processes underlying the illness affecting both mind and body that characterises each child's state of (un)wellness.

Yoga is a traditional practice that helps maintain good health. Throughout the world, people are seeking to appreciate the principles of yoga with the aim of improving the quality of their lives. The word 'yoga' comes from the Sanskrit root 'yuj' which means 'to join' or 'to yoke'. The main goal in yoga is to achieve the union of mind with body, as physical health is inextricably interlinked with clarity of mind. This chapter seeks to present the hypothesis that a perfect medical consultation involves a fuller appreciation of the mind and body, and the link between mind and body in each of our patients. This appreciation may then empower us to identify the components of each child's dis-ease, unique for each individual, leading to a more holistic, yet personalised, management plan for each child that should result in better long-term management.

Children and adults continue to die from asthma attacks. Many others continue to suffer from asthma for weeks through every year.

Children miss school, adults miss work, the NHS and other healthcare systems elsewhere in the world are reeling under the burden of acute asthma. Is this because science does not have the answers to the health problems of asthma? Alternatively, is this, at least in part, because of our unfinished consultations, the unfinished aspects preventing us from drawing a more complete picture of the illnesses affecting individuals?

References and further reading

Basu, K., Palmer, C.N., Tavendale, R., Lipworth, B.J. and Mukhopadhyay, S. (2009) 'Adrenergic beta(2)-receptor genotype predisposes to exacerbations in steroid-treated asthmatic patients taking frequent albuterol or salmeterol.' *Journal of Allergy and Clinical Immunology* 124, 6, 1188–1194.

Basu, K., Palmer, C.N.A., Lipworth, B. J., McLean, W.H., Terron-Kwiatkowski, A., Zhao, Y., *et al.* (2008) 'Filaggrin null mutations are associated with increased asthma exacerbations in children and young adults.' *Allergy* 63, 9, 1211–1217.

Bisgaard, H., Simpson, A., Palmer, C.N.A., Bønnelykke, K., Mclean, I., Mukhopadhyay, S., *et al.* (2008) 'Gene-environment interaction in the penetrance of eczema in infancy replicated in two birth-cohort studies: Filaggrin loss-of-function mutations triggered by cat exposure.' *PLOS Medicine* 24 June, 5, 6, e131.

Brown, K.W., West, A.M., Loverich, T.M. and Biegel, G.M. (2011) 'Assessing adolescent mindfulness: Validation of an adapted Mindful Attention Awareness Scale in adolescent normative and psychiatric populations.' *Psychological Assessment* 23, 4, 1023–1033.

Henderson, J., Northstone, K., Lee, S., Liao, H., Zhao, Y., Pembrey, M., *et al.* (2008) 'The burden of disease associated with filaggrin mutations: A population based, longitudinal birth cohort study.' *Journal of Allergy and Clinical Immunology* 121, 4, 872–877.

Mukhopadhyay, S., Sypek, J., Tavendale, R., Gartner, U., Winter, J., Li, W., *et al.* (2010) 'Matrix metalloproteinase-12 is a therapeutic target for asthma in children and young adults.' *Journal of Allergy and Clinical Immunology* 126, 70–76.

Palmer, C.N.A., Lipworth, B., Lee, S., Ismail, T., Macgregor, D.F. and Mukhopadhyay, S. (2006) 'The Arg16 β2 receptor genotype increases exacerbation risk in children with asthma on salmeterol.' *Thorax* 61, 940–944.

Palmer, C.N.A., Irvine, A.D., Terron-Kwiatkowski, A., Zhao, Y., Liao, H., Lee, S.P., *et al.* (2006) 'Common loss-of-function variants of the epidermal barrier protein filaggrin are a major predisposing factor for atopic dermatitis.' *Nature Genetics* 38, 4, 441–446.

Palmer, C.N., Ismail, T., Lee, S.P., Terron-Kwiatkowski, A., Zhao, Y., Liao, H., *et al.* (2007) 'Filaggrin null mutations are associated with increased asthma severity in children and young adults.' *Journal of Allergy and Clinical Immunology* 120, 1, 64–68.

Yoga.org.nz (no date) 'Definition of yoga.' Available at http://yoga.org.nz/what-is-yoga/yoga_definition.htm, accessed on 10 January 2017.

7

Radiotherapy – Head and Neck

CHICKENS OR NUNS: WORKING OUT WHAT IS IMPORTANT

Pat Shields

Pat Shields qualified as a therapy radiographer at Hammersmith Hospital, London. Over the years, she has worked in many of the teaching hospitals in London, both in oncology and nuclear medicine. On moving north, she worked at the Christie NHS Foundation Trust in Manchester and Clatterbridge Cancer Centre NHS Trust in Liverpool, and also spent time working in Beirut and Hong Kong. She has most recently worked at the Royal Sussex County Hospital in Brighton for 23 years, the last 16 years as a Macmillan head and neck specialist radiographer. Her enthusiasm has always been for patient-centred holistic care. She will soon be retiring after 43 years as a therapy radiographer.

I never wanted to work in a hospital. I had no desire to help others in a professional way, and no wish to spend my day in a smelly, antiseptic environment or be trapped in a uniform all day. I came from a small mining village on the East Coast of Scotland, and all I wanted was to be a fashion designer. I had three options: the woollen mill with all the wool you could knit; the chicken factory with all the chicken you could eat; or, as a special treat, as I was clever, I could go to the Catholic Teacher Training College, stay with the nuns, abide by their rules and stay behind locked doors for four years. My response to all three: help!

I was 19, young and optimistic, and the answer was obvious: all roads led to London. Drawing, sewing and making clothes were my only ambitions so, with hardly a backward glance towards my seven siblings, off I went.

In spite of old photographs, 1972 was a difficult time in Britain: three-day working week, limited electricity for everyone, high unemployment. Edward Heath was the Prime Minister. My parents asked me to compromise and complete a training course that would give me prospects for the future, and then I could go to fashion college afterwards. My best subjects were physics, maths and art. I decided to train as a therapy radiographer. It wouldn't matter if I didn't like it as it would be temporary. I hated everything about it, not only the smells, but also the patients and the uniform.

One day everything changed as a result of something quite ordinary, when as a student I listened to the consultant oncologist tell an old lady that she just needed a few treatments and everything would be all right. This lady had a fungating breast tumour and would obviously be leaving our beautiful planet after not too long. My whole being screamed silently – how could this be happening? She had things to attend to, and instead of being helped, she was being removed from the truth that would enable her to say goodbye to her family, write a will and prepare herself in whatever way she saw fit for the next life, if she believed in one.

The consultant oncologist was a kind, thoughtful man of his time, a time when the word cancer was rarely said out loud, and certainly not within hearing distance of patients who definitely did not need to know everything or have an opinion on their care. Back then we treated the disease, not the person, but all that has changed – hasn't it? We would all like to treat the whole person and not just the disease that lies within their physical body but, with time constraints, ever-increasing numbers of patients and the beating stick of targets, it is difficult. Treating the disease and not the patient is easier and quicker. It is not the answer if we want to heal the sick. Those moments in the consulting room have stayed with me for over 40 years.

It was many years before the role of information and support radiographer was introduced, but with the help of my manager and Macmillan we got the post up and running. At last I could look after the whole person and not think only of the cancer hidden within. I started in this position 16 years ago. There were very few of us then, no guidelines to follow, no one to teach us what to do. We had to make it up as we went along.

As information and support radiographer, my job was to ensure that all patients in the Sussex Cancer Centre who were having radiotherapy had the support and information they needed. This would not be possible now, but there were fewer patients then and, rightly or wrongly, they were less demanding. Hard to imagine that there were very few information leaflets, and most were made by well-meaning staff in their own time.

Within the first year of supporting the patients, it became obvious to me that the patients with head and neck cancer needed so much more care than the other groups of patients. A quick audit showed that 10 per cent of the patients needed 90 per cent of my time. It was also obvious to me that I did not know how to care for them. I did not know enough about the diagnosis, treatment and side-effects of treatment to look after this complex group of patients. I had climbed into a hole that I needed to get out of. I felt useless.

As far as I knew, no one else was doing this specific job, so once more, no written instructions, no one to learn from. I needed to become a specialist if I was going to be useful. With the help of my manager and invaluable instruction and encouragement from Dr George Deutsch, consultant oncologist, my apprenticeship began. For the last 15 years I have been the keyworker for patients with head and neck cancer while they are having radiotherapy, with or without additional chemotherapy. I continue my apprenticeship every day working with patients and the amazing team in oncology.

Head and neck cancers are a group of approximately 16 different cancers, all situated between the eyebrows and the top of the oesophagus (thyroid and parathyroid are not included). These cancers are rare, in total approximately only 10 per cent of all cancers. A GP is likely to see only one in their professional life. They are difficult to diagnose and treat. Due to the aetiology of head and neck cancers, there is a higher percentage of alcoholics and drug users than in other cancer groups, which can add to the challenge of caring for this group of patients.

In oncology, treatment is normally six weeks of daily radiotherapy with the addition of weekly chemotherapy. The side effects are cumulative and are at their peak two weeks after treatment has been completed. These side-effects can be horrendous and at times life-threatening. Patients often come to the Cancer Centre for treatment after extensive and sometimes disfiguring surgery, perhaps having had a laryngectomy or their tongue removed. It is important that radiotherapy follows within six weeks of surgery even if patients do not have time to make full recovery from surgery before they face weeks of pain, nausea, difficulty with eating, swallowing and even talking. All of this on top of the shock of a cancer diagnosis, perhaps with the added anxiety of not being able to return to work or pay the mortgage or having to find money to pay for an 80-mile round trip each day. Normal daily family routines are totally disrupted.

This puts a terrible strain not only on the patient, but also on all of their family members and close friends. Most treatments are delivered with curative intent and the patients are successfully cured, but for some unfortunate patients, palliation of symptoms is the only option. While going through the treatment, the patient is cared for in specific ways by different members of the multidisciplinary support team that includes specialist nurses, a speech and language therapist and a dietician.

My job as the keyworker is to look after the whole person. I am with the consultant oncologist when the patient is given confirmation of their cancer diagnosis, and treatment options are discussed and agreed upon. Then I spend time alone with the patient, and my aim at that time is to create rapport and a bond of trust. My technique is one of honest and direct communication. Sometimes this takes the patient unawares, but almost without exception after the treatment is complete, patients tell me how helpful my honest approach has been.

Here are some things I might ask:

- How come you are an alcoholic?
- Why are you feeling so aggressive?
- What happened to make you homeless?
- Why are you so afraid of death?
- Tell me, do you believe in God?
- Are you afraid of death or dying?

This approach is blunt and, some might say, very Scottish, but it works because I want to know the answers. Every one of us enjoys telling our story and being listened to. These questions give the patient the opportunity to tell their story, which is an essential part of the healing process. Perhaps the financial cost in appeasing disgruntled patients might be reduced if their story had been heard before hospital disaster struck.

I see patients weekly in an on-treatment clinic to assess and manage the side-effects. Regularly there are over 20 patients to be seen, each one of them deserving undivided attention. Seeing one patient after the other all day long with barely time for lunch is exhausting but deeply satisfying. Addressing their individual problems and allowing them to feel safe in a 15-minute slot is a challenge but not insurmountable. Having spent time getting to know them and creating a rapport before treatment starts makes the task immeasurably easier and allows me to treat them all as individuals.

We all want to treat patients as individuals, but as we struggle to work within the straightjacket of guidelines, political correctness and impossible targets sent down from on high, we are robbed of the ability to make decisions or independent judgements which, in turn, makes us resentful, unhappy and stressed. We are not supposed to give a patient a hug when that is all they need at that moment, for fear of being condescending. We may misread the signs or call an old lady 'dear'. Stress, like happiness, is contagious, and unfortunately the former is spreading like wildfire through the NHS.

Love yourself

Self-care is the cornerstone of patient care. Caring for the patient, body and soul, comes second to caring for ourselves. We, the carers, have to come back another day, and another, and again, for many years. Caring for ourselves gives us core strength and allows us to be the same balanced person, both in and out of working hours. My release is creative needlework and mosaic art. When I am in my art room time stands still, four hours pass in the blink of an eye. There is total absorption and a spiritual connection, a feeling of being connected to something greater than myself. I have come to understand that time spent in my art room is not a luxury but a necessity. Without this time my life becomes more difficult, more stressful and more frustrating. This is what feeds my spirit and lights my fire. I went to fashion college and in my spare time I design and create unusual wedding dresses – the last one was a black extravaganza for a Goth.

Just listening

We need to know what feeds the spirit of the patient, but how do we find out? Easy: here is the key. Just ask, then listen. 'Tell me your story' leads to the most interesting and unexpected conversations and adds immeasurably to the bond of trust. Most recently I listened to the stories of an active environmentalist, a stunt man, a lady who uses handmade paper to bind books on a machine invented in the 1400s, a passionate baker, an alcoholic whose father hated him so much he would push the three-year-old's fingers into the open fire just for fun. I once looked after a transsexual who bred rare pigs, and we chatted about the pigs, not his cancer.

In listening to these stories, everything changes in the telling. The patient forgets that they are in the cancer centre. They light up, and for that short time, the cancer does not exist in their bodies. After listening, it would be impossible not to feel deep compassion for a human being who is walking on the planet at the same time as myself; impossible not to do whatever I can to ease their suffering. A deep bond is forged and all of this in ten minutes. Listening to stories opens the door to a deeper understanding of the person in whom the cancer exists, and gives us an insight into what soul or spirit might mean to them. It creates a spiritual connection. Listening is a powerful and underused tool.

In the pub

I run a support group for patients and their partners or carers. We are a 40-strong group who support and care for each other (yes, they care for me too). Quite often our meetings are in the pub, and over eight years close friendships have been formed. I thought it would be interesting to present them with a questionnaire, which I do not have time for during the working day. I am interested in the meaning of life and how it differs with different individuals, and wondered how this might change with a cancer diagnosis and if and when they were given the all clear. My plan was to speak to 20 patients but I stopped after only 10, as the answers I was given were so surprising and moving.

I gave each person a short list of questions, and a week later I spent about an hour chatting through their responses:

> Did a cancer diagnosis change meaning in your life? If yes, in what way?

> Did being cured of cancer change meaning in your life? If yes, in what way?

Or:

> Has knowing that your cancer will not be cured and you will die of this disease changed meaning in your life? If so, in what way?

In spite of the fact that I had seen these patients through treatment, had listened to their stories and thought I had known them well for up to eight years, their replies revealed so much more. I was astounded. Most of them spoke of a deep well of gratitude to the NHS and staff. They spoke of the exquisite beauty of the planet, the miracle of a blade of grass and the deep joy of a sunrise or a sunset. Some felt that most of their friends and family walked through life with their eyes shut, worrying about things that don't matter, but they also felt that it would be difficult to explain their new emotions.

How could I not have noticed that one of them had tried to commit suicide during treatment? This man had been rude, difficult and non-compliant. He now told me that he felt that he had deserved to die as a punishment for his heavy smoking and drinking, and for being a useless husband and father. He had written a suicide note and was preparing to jump from a great height when he had a moment of clarity and decided to try to make reparation by being the good husband and father he had never been. I am happy to say he is now sober, in a happy marriage, and has an especially deep love for his grandchildren.

Then there was a dying patient who felt that, by overcoming his alcoholism and drug addiction, that he had cleared his karma, so he would be happy to let go and look forward to his next life, which he felt would be a happy one. All of this in spite of the fact that 18 months previously a scan showed that his cancer had been cured.

I would have missed these stories if I had not taken the time to listen. They are clear examples of the spirit as well as the body being addressed and given the opportunity to heal. The process was synergistic, for their open and honest replies fed my spirit, filling up the love tank. As my mother used to say, 'let's walk in the woods and fill up the love tank'. She has been dead for almost 40 years, but I still pay heed, and try to keep the tank topped up.

All of those I spoke to felt that the process of answering the questions was healing, and three of the ten felt that all patients should be given time to reflect on their period of threatening illness. One of them felt that addressing the questions and chatting through the answers had brought him peace of mind that he had not had for four years since his treatment had finished. No one had asked them these questions before, and it's not really an easy conversation for the dinner table. Some said that they could not have shared their thoughts with loved ones for fear of upset, or they felt that their newly acquired depth of feeling and emotion might cause a division. Ordinary life now seemed magical.

You might like to hear some of the things that they said:

The world is a shinier place.

Every human looks beautiful to me.

I am bursting to tell people the joy I feel, but I am not sure they would understand.

The love I feel for my wife and family is immeasurably deeper than it was.

Listening to all of this has changed my practice. I now ask patients at the beginning of treatment what it is that will get them through it. At first, they don't understand. I ask, 'Why do you want to live?' 'What lights your fire? 'What will give you the determination to keep going when things get tough?' This helps me focus my encouragement on the patient as an individual. For example, for one lady it was her son's wedding that was in the middle of treatment, and she feared she would miss it. I reorganised her appointments and arranged for her to have a makeover before the big day.

An elderly man felt that he could not have treatment as he was the main carer for his wife who had Alzheimer's disease. We discussed the option of him having late appointments so that he could settle her before leaving for the hospital. The treatment radiographers obliged by sneaking him to the top of the queue each day so that his time away from his wife was kept to a minimum.

Gestures don't need to be grand. A simple comment, an easy smile can work little miracles:

Is that a new scarf? I haven't seen it before.

How did your granddaughter cope with her first day at school?

You look very sad today. Would a chat help?

What makes your heart sing?

A patient started treatment recently, a writer whose anxiety levels were so high they were almost palpable. We chatted about what was important to him, what made his heart sing. Playing classical pieces on the piano was his answer. We agreed that an hour each day of practice, particularly complicated pieces, might help. An hour each day when the cancer did not exist, and he could be connected to his spirit, could only help with his anxiety. I listened to Chopin in the evening, but did not let him know that I prefer Dolly Parton!

Two patients told me of how a simple but generous gesture could, even after 40 years, bring them to tears. A 90-year-old man who had been a fighter pilot in the Second World War and then an exhibition motorcyclist told me he was afraid of nothing. I commented that he looked very anxious to me, sweating, wringing his hands and with shallow breathing. He said his only fear was hospitals and asked if he could tell me a story. 'Many years ago I had to have a small cancer, which was on my face near my eye, removed by local anaesthetic. Apart from the surgeon, there were about five other people in the room, just shadows around me. I was terrified as the surgeon came at me with a knife. One of the shadows came towards me, a nurse. I remember she was plump and had a gorgeous smile. She said that she would take my hand and not let go until it was all over. I instantly felt safe and have not forgotten her.' The second was an ex-patient, a woman in her 70s. She related the story of how 30 years previously she was due to have her bladder removed as a result of cancer. At 5am on the scheduled date the surgeon came to her bedside and woke her saying he had come to see her and reassure her, saying, 'I will do your surgery today, you mustn't worry, everything will be all right.' She believed him, and it was.

After decades, both of them had tears in their eyes as they remembered how deeply they had been moved by these acts of kindness when they felt vulnerable and lonely. We talk about going the extra mile, but if we are going to measure it, a few centimetres does the trick. In both cases a pure and deep spiritual connection was made, and this is what brought tears not only to their eyes but also to mine as I witnessed their deep emotion.

Filling up the love tank

When we feel love and kindness to others, it not only makes others feel loved and cared for but it helps us to develop inner happiness and peace. (Dalai Lama)

Treating the patient, body, mind and spirit, as a complete human being has many benefits for their care. So in taking care of others, we are taking care of ourselves, filling up the love tank. We all help others every day. We do it without thinking and without understanding the great impact it has on the lives of others. Small acts of kindness can stay lodged in people's hearts and have the strength to bring tears to their eyes 30 years later. For us, the carers, it is no different. Kind words, acts or stories from a patient stay with us forever, become part of our fibre, form our very being.

Things I remember. In 1973 Mrs Bradbury gave me a red rose the night before she died. The father who brought his child from Greece to be cured of leukaemia sent me cards and small gifts for 15 years. I imagine and hope that Luca, the small bewildered child who spoke no English, is now a happy grandfather.

My last story is very sweet and moving. A 92-year-old lady was offered radiotherapy to palliate her advanced cancer which, untreated, would most likely cause her death within a few months. She attended with her two daughters who were very keen for her to have treatment as, understandably, they wanted her to live for as long as possible. I could see that the patient was not so keen so I asked her family if they would like to have a coffee while I spent some time alone with her. On their return, they found us both roaring with laughter. I had asked the old lady if she thought she might go to heaven when she died. She replied that she was tired, had had a good life and was indeed looking forward to it. 'Anyone up there waiting for you? A husband perhaps?' 'Well that's the problem. There are three of them. I will be darting between the clouds avoiding them.' What a picture that makes. We are all blessed to be able listen to these stories, to have them become part of who we are, to stay with us forever. This is what sustains us, gives us the energy to continue caring, fills up our love tank.

8

Dementia

HOW THE HUMANITIES CAN HELP US CONFRONT THE DEMONS OF PRACTICE

Muna Al-Jawad

Muna Al-Jawad, MBBS, FRCP, MA Clinical Education, is a consultant geriatrician who works at the Royal Sussex County Hospital in Brighton. As well as her day-to-day work as a doctor, she is interested in using comics as a practitioner research method.

People who know me were surprised when I said I was doing this. One of my friends actually scoffed at the idea of me being spiritual. To be honest, I was quite taken aback when Peter asked me to contribute to a book on the subject of spirituality. I am a lifelong atheist, definitely not a hippie – I don't even like mindfulness. The closest I have come to a 'religious experience' was seeing Björk perform at a music festival and feeling carried away by the music, lyrics and movement of the crowd.

I am a consultant in geriatric medicine. I mainly work on a ward in the general hospital that specialises in providing care for people who have an acute medical problem and an additional need as a result of dementia or delirium. I've been a doctor for about 15 years at the time of writing. I am also a comics artist. One of the reasons I draw comics is to express the intangible (some might say, spiritual) aspects of practice.

In this chapter I am going to use Lynda Barry's concept of autobio-fictionalography to express myself and explore the issues (Barry 2002).

I will frame my experiences and memories around six demons. These represent areas of difficulty, uncertainty or doubt, where perhaps a spiritual or less 'clinical' perspective might be required.

So if you want expertise and definitions, turn to the next chapter. All I can offer is a personal perspective on my practice in healthcare. I will use my point of view (and my comics) to try to explore:

- What does spirituality mean to me, working in dementia care?
- How can understanding spiritual aspects of healthcare make a difference to practitioners and to patients?

It's time to begin with my first demon, Disconnection.

Our expectation is that healthcare professionals will be empathic and compassionate, that they will really care about their patients. This is actually very difficult to do. The emotional labour required of us, day in day out, potentially for many years, can easily lead to burnout (Theodosius 2008). However well intentioned we are, healthcare workers are human, we have feelings, and these may not always be positive, nurturing feelings.

One option to defend against uncomfortable emotions is to disconnect. I can do my job well enough even on a bad day. The zombie version of me can keep patients safe and appear to make adequate clinical decisions. Sometimes we have to disconnect to do what would otherwise be unthinkable – make a 98-year-old lady scream by stabbing her with a needle, for example. The world of the hospital can be violent and inhumane; no one can be truly 'connected' to a place like this for very long.

So how do we reconnect? Just telling us to be more compassionate doesn't work – most staff want to act with compassion, but we need to enable ourselves to do this. One way is through music.

* Behuniak (2011)

On my ward, we are interested in personalised music for people with dementia. We have musicians who visit the ward once a week, go from patient to patient, spending time with each person to play their favourites. Our intention was to do something good, something healing for patients: to allow them to access memories that are otherwise inaccessible, and to connect emotionally with the world. It does work: people wake up, they join in, there are often smiles and tears.

What is interesting is that the music affects staff too. Personally, I can't help joining in. I sway or quietly hum along. I feel calmer and happier in my work, I feel more connected with my patients and the other people who work on the ward. Music is intensely personal yet somehow universal. We stop being just doctors, nurses and patients, we stop being zombies, we become human.

There are risks to dropping my guard and becoming more human. I sometimes have to leave the ward during the music sessions. Sometimes I feel so connected to the tragic stories of some of my patients that sadness and grief overwhelm me. I retreat to the safety of my office and mundane emails. Music is a potent force to be used wisely in healthcare. It reminds us that there is more to life than metal bed frames, intravenous lines and bodies under sheets. It connects us to each other. I think what this demon is trying to say is that spirituality is connectedness with other people.

A particularly isolating time for me is on the night shift. My next demon is Darkness.

Most hospital-based TV programmes are set in the Emergency Department, where the lights are always bright, where there is lots of noise and drama. It surprised me when I first started working as a doctor that the rest of the hospital is pretty dark at night. Most corridors are lit, but the wards themselves generally encourage sleep by having the lights off or down very low. This makes sense. Of course people need sleep to get better, but for me it can make things seem pretty bleak.

I remember nights on the wards very well from my time as a junior doctor. The solitary light from the nurses' station, whispered voices of

Darkness

Demon #2

For me, the worst time in hospital is between 2am and dawn

Your judgement is impaired by tiredness and nausea

Artificial light makes everything seem a bit unreal

It's easy to feel you are the only healthy person left in the world

The stories mostly aren't funny or glamorous so I tend not to bore friends with them

The darkness still scares me and the guilt remains with me but the main thing is...

... I survived.

concern, trying to assess someone half-lit, half-asleep, all added to the feeling of uneasiness that night brings. Knowing I was probably the only doctor awake, and to ask for help would mean waking someone up from precious sleep, only made me feel more isolated. Decision-making is difficult in these circumstances; even working out how worried to be is tricky. I have stood outside at dawn (usually in the hospital car park), wondering if I did the right thing, feeling guilty for what I did or didn't decide to do. Things are clearer in the day time, in retrospect and when discussed with colleagues.

So what sees us through the dark nights? Food? (I was once told that calories don't count on nights!) The promise of sleep when it's all over? The thought of being out of the hospital with friends or family who are not ill? Perhaps the classic image is a good one. Spirituality is whatever gives you light on a dark night.

Like me, people with dementia can sometimes get more confused and disorientated at night. This phenomenon is called 'sun downing'. To think about how we deal with these and other symptoms, my third demon is Distress.

People with dementia can have difficulty expressing themselves and explaining what is wrong. Especially when physically unwell, they are at risk of developing a condition called delirium, where they become more confused and disorientated. This can mean someone is drowsy or it can mean they are hyper-alert. There are sometimes other symptoms: walking around, apparently without purpose, physically or verbally challenging people they don't recognise or remember, calling out for help.

All of these things are commonly witnessed on hospital wards, including the ward I work on currently. It is very hard to work when someone is constantly screaming, but you can get used to it and stop hearing it as a call for help. It can be frustrating when there is no obvious cause for the person's cries. It often annoys other patients and relatives. It is upsetting for relatives to see their loved one in such a state.

The language we use betrays a lot about how we interpret these symptoms in our practice. It is commonplace to hear words such as

'agitated' or 'aggressive' when describing patients' behaviours. Clearly no one would want to be described in these terms themselves, and so alternatives need to be found. I have been guilty of using such language myself in the past. Through thinking hard about what language means and with guidance from senior nursing colleagues, I changed my use of language and referred to 'challenging behaviour'. This term has found favour as it is not pejorative and it puts the focus on staff to manage the behaviour rather than blame the person for how they are.

However, this focus on 'managing behaviour' can lead to a tendency to do just that, without thinking about what might lie behind the symptoms. So we sedate, or restrain, or reassure without making a diagnosis or working out why the behaviour is present.

The latest thinking in dementia care is to refer to these symptoms as 'distress' (DSDC no date). This feels like the right word to use as it emphasises the need to look for a cause for distress (be that physical, mental or spiritual anguish) and address it. It makes us think of behaviour as a form of communication and use observed patterns or cues to work out what is underlying the person's distress in order to alleviate it.

In this context spirituality might be about moving beyond behaviour and the purely physical world to why the person might be upset and addressing an unmet need.

The next demon is Disorientation and might help us think further about unmet need and how to address it.

It's easy to pity people who are disorientated. After all, it can lead to misunderstandings and sometimes distress. However, I think we can become too concerned with the need to be constantly aware of 'reality'. Most people have probably been disorientated at one time or another, through illness, medications, anaesthetic or other substances, and it isn't always unpleasant. In fact some people actively seek out a different experience of reality for recreational purposes. There are various philosophical schools of thought that reality is essentially constructed by our own experiences, sensations and consciousness (Bruner 1987). Even visceral sensations such as the pain of hitting your hand with a

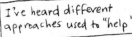

hammer can be altered by what else is going on in the moment. The stories we tell may well be the most truthful version of reality there is, as these are obviously constructed by us and don't pretend otherwise.

However relaxed we feel about what reality is, it can be hard to know how to respond to someone who is convinced they know what is going on and will not accept the 'true' version of events. One of the commonest questions I'm asked in practice and in education sessions is the right way to respond in these circumstances.

The answer, of course, is 'it depends'. It depends on what the person with dementia needs, what they are trying to tell you and what the purpose of your conversation is. It may be very important that the person understands they have cancer as they need to help make a decision about the best course of treatment. In this case it would be right to attempt reorientation to person and place to give them the best chance of deciding. However, if the person is attempting to leave the ward because they think they are late for work, they may not believe you when you tell them they are a patient in a hospital, despite all the visible evidence. It may be better to try distraction and reassurance. Anxiety about lateness might be an expression of a different underlying worry.

Some centres go further and construct whole other realities for people with dementia. There are wards with bus stops for people to wait at, there are reminiscence rooms decorated in 1950s wallpaper and furniture, there are whole villages with fake post offices and post office workers who are really carers. Although these might feel uncomfortable (because the bus never comes and the letters never get there), how far you venture into constructing new realities is, I think, dependent on what works for the person with dementia you care for. For me, as long as the new reality works for the person with dementia, and doesn't cause further distress in the longer term, it's probably okay.

Looking after people who are disorientated makes me think that perhaps spirituality is accepting other people's realities.

Considering there are no hard and fast rules about how to respond to disorientation, perhaps we need to question the places of rules in healthcare more generally. The fifth demon is Dogma.

* Al-Jawad and Frost (2014)

Hospitals can be interesting and fun places to work, but sometimes we are stifled by rules and policies. There is a culture of accepting the rules and adhering to them whenever possible. Rules are there for a reason, after all, often to keep people safe. There are also some unwritten rules or dogma that can be helpful to make life on the ward work smoothly (for example, never sit in the ward clerk's chair), but there are others that can be unhelpful (for example, all patients should be up and washed before doctors' rounds). There is also a natural human culture of subversion. If we are told we can't do something and we think it's important, we sometimes find a way to work around the rules. Sometimes, if it's really important, we break the rules.

On our ward, we are subject to the same Trust policies, safety orders, quality standards and audit reports as everyone else. We also make an effort to allow staff on the ward to do things a bit differently. Ideas are discussed on a weekly basis about how we might make things better for patients and for ourselves. This rarely involves making new rules. It does involve working out what is important to us and to our patients, and balancing this against safety concerns. This reassessment of risk is what, I think, we do well on the ward. Of course a knitting needle could be a dangerous weapon in the wrong hands, but this much loved activity can keep someone happy, calm and occupied, leading to less distress and improved quality of life.

We created a manifesto on our unit. We don't break rules for the sake of it. We embrace creativity and open discussion of risk and priorities in an effort to allow both staff and patients to flourish. It doesn't always work, we sometimes get it wrong and we accept this. Perhaps spirituality is breaking the rules.

My last demon is perhaps the biggest demon of all, Death.

My first job as a doctor was as a house officer in surgery. People didn't die very often on surgical wards and when they did, it was quite a big deal, especially if they had had an operation. We had mortality meetings where the senior doctors talked about these deaths and whether they could have been avoided. After six months I moved to medicine. The

medical wards, particularly the elderly care wards, were full of death, accepted as normal, hardly discussed. It was a bit of a shock, I suppose.

I was 24 when I qualified as a doctor and I hadn't seen very many dead people before. There were cadavers that we dissected at medical school, an important rite of passage, but in the sterile and formaldehyde-filled anatomy department, somehow disconnected from real life. I was a fifth year student when my grandma died. She looked asleep, at peace and no longer suffering. Seeing her body didn't upset me. What was more difficult was the loss for my family and thinking about the effect of this on all of us.

Healthcare workers early in their careers may not have had much exposure to death. Our culture keeps children and younger people sheltered from the physical reality of the dying and dead. This means that people may not know what to expect, which might lead to anxiety around caring for dying people or what happens after death.

Nowadays, I don't generally feel sad for the dead person but I still feel the relatives' sense of loss. The most upsetting deaths for me, now, are where the family members are very distressed or finding the grief difficult to manage. This can be hard for everyone on the ward, and we try and debrief when a death has affected us.

There is no doubt that our personal experiences impact on our feelings in our work as healthcare professionals. Remembering this and supporting each other can make the hard times bearable. Spirituality is looking after ourselves and each other.

Conclusion

Having considered my six demons, I conclude this chapter by going back to my original questions.

WHAT DOES SPIRITUALITY MEAN TO ME, WORKING IN DEMENTIA CARE?

Choosing these six areas of practice to focus on has shown me six possible meanings of spirituality in my practice. Spirituality is connectedness with other people. Spirituality is whatever gives you light on a dark night. Spirituality is about moving beyond behaviour to addressing an unmet need. Spirituality is accepting other people's realities. Spirituality is breaking the rules. Spirituality is looking after ourselves and each other.

These are very personal and specific to my work in dementia care, but may, perhaps, have some meaning for others.

HOW CAN UNDERSTANDING SPIRITUAL ASPECTS OF HEALTHCARE MAKE A DIFFERENCE TO PRACTITIONERS AND TO PATIENTS?

Hospital wards can be brutal and inhumane places. It is essential that staff are given a way to resist this inhumanity (Shem 2002). Art, music and the humanities more generally are the ways I resist becoming a zombie and connect with the spiritual aspects of my practice. The demons will always be with me, but at least this way I can think about them and come to some kind of understanding of them. It is important to make opportunities for healthcare practitioners to be spiritual in their own way. This might be through talking, writing, drawing or just reflecting on practice. Allowing practitioners to flourish in this way means care is more likely to be connected, compassionate and person-centred. Patients and their relatives can only benefit from this too.

References

Al-Jawad, M. and Frost, L. (2014) 'Creating and analysing practitioner comics to develop a meaningful ward manifesto for a new dementia care unit.' *International Practice Development Journal* 4, 2.

Barry, L. (2002) *One Hundred Demons*. Seattle, WA: Sasquatch Books.

Behuniak, S.M. (2011) 'The living dead? The construction of people with Alzheimer's disease as zombies.' *Ageing & Society* 31, 70–92.

Bruner, J. (1987) 'Life as narrative.' *Social Research* 54, 11–32.

DSDC (Dementia Services Development Centre) (no date) *Understanding Distressed Behaviour*. Available at http://dementia.stir.ac.uk/education/training-directory/ understanding-distressed-behaviour, accessed on 26 September 2016.

Kay, J. (2011) *Red Dust Road*. London: Picador.

Shem, S. (2002) 'Fiction as resistance.' *Annals of Internal Medicine* 137, 934–937.

Theodosius, C. (2008) *Emotional Labour in Health Care: The Unmanaged Heart of Nursing*. London: Routledge.

9

Renal

ADVANCED KIDNEY DISEASE

Adam MacDiarmaid-Gordon

Dr Adam MacDiarmaid-Gordon, MBChB (Hons), FRCP, qualified from Liverpool University in 1984 and trained in Liverpool, Manchester and the Midlands. He became a consultant in Renal Medicine in Brighton in 1999. He is a fellow of the Royal College of Physicians and a full time Renal Physician, managing patients approaching or receiving dialysis. He is on the editorial board of Clinical Ethics and has published on clinical ethics.

This has not been easy to write despite the repeated encouragement from (and tolerance by) Peter Wells. I have struggled to identify what it is that I do that has led to my being asked to contribute this chapter. If there is a simple spectrum of practice with protocol-based medicine at one end and a highly personalised medicine at the other, then I am probably closer to the latter than the former. Having said that, I am not convinced that simple linearity describes practice. My close experience of other doctors is largely my experience of colleagues in our department and our Trust, not necessarily representative of doctors as a whole. This will therefore be personal, not too personal I hope, which I think is what was asked of me.

What I cover here is a complex form of therapy involving doctors, nurses, dieticians, pharmacists and, for some patients, counsellors. I am not the only person involved even in decision-making, far less in providing treatment. That must be recognised, and hence some of what follows is a description of processes. Any ability I have to minimise the effects of treatment of kidney disease on a patient's ability to live life to the best they can is dependent on our unit as a whole (and the wider health service) to offer as wide a range of treatments as possible; without that range there can be no choice.

A little about me first: I am a consultant nephrologist (otherwise called a renal physician), that is to say, I specialise in diseases of the kidneys. I have been a consultant for nearly two decades and a doctor since the mid-1980s. My practice has been entirely in the UK. In a book, the title of which includes the word 'soul' and which is edited by a priest, it seems appropriate to describe my own position. I was brought up as an Anglican and regard myself as such, although I don't manifest that strongly and am far from devout. I don't presume to understand God's intent, and imagine He may accept each of us as we are, regardless of our faith or lack of it.

My understanding of the word 'soul' as we are to use it in this context is not one rooted in religion. Rather, I am advised to consider what things give meaning or value to people's lives (by their estimation), something like a raison d'être or possibly, at times, a personal event they do not wish to miss. That simplifies things as, although I am aware of some of the ways in which religious faith of different sorts might interact with health and medicine or healthcare, my direct involvement is from my professional background. This may be almost 'mechanical' or impersonal; for example, a simple awareness of religious fasting and its effects on the treatments we provide. I do not see it as appropriate, certainly not my role, to engage in unsolicited and inadequately informed spiritual discussions with patients whose own focus when they see me is their health. To be aware of faiths and their influence on health is essential; to encroach on the former when your role is the latter is something else. So when I consider 'soul' here, it is in a secular way or in a way that generalises beyond a specific faith. The issue is how we intrude on life as little as possible, allowing space for life to be lived as close to how it would be were the person not a patient.

A little about kidney disease and its treatment is relevant here. I focus on patients with advanced kidney disease, partly because, within the range of renal medicine, that area is a large part of my personal practice, and because that is the area where the issues I have been asked to consider are highly relevant, if not always visible.

By advanced kidney disease (what used to be called kidney failure), I mean the long-term and irreversible loss of kidney function to the level where patients are becoming ill from that, and who face the prospect of life-changing treatments or of dying from kidney failure. It is not common. I don't think this is a place for lots of numbers or statistics: suffice it to say, our unit has a catchment area of around 1.3 million, with 4–500 patients on dialysis and a similar number of patients who have transplants (most of whom will have had dialysis at some stage). In common with many other diseases, partly because it is often a complication of those diseases, it is more prevalent in old age and in people from minority ethnic groups. The effects of social deprivation and rural vs. urban lifestyle on renal disease are complicated by their impact on access to healthcare. Our unit in the South East of England is not extreme in any of these contexts, hence my comments should be generalisable. The model for renal care through most of the UK is hub-and-spoke, with big multi-professional renal teams based in large or teaching hospitals providing outreach clinics and other services in local hospitals or other settings.

The kidneys have an inexplicable amount of functional reserve: a large amount of kidney function can be lost without it being obvious to the patient. Many patients with milder degrees of kidney disease will only be aware of it because of the results of a blood test done for other reasons or because they have a condition, such as diabetes, which causes kidney disease sufficiently often to make routine surveillance for it appropriate. For many patients, providing that they have at least 30 per cent of kidney function, much, if not all, of their care can be provided with only a small amount of direct involvement from their renal unit. At levels below that, more involvement is needed both to manage the renal disease itself and to prepare for later stages such as dialysis. The point at which patients develop symptoms due to 'kidney failure' (as distinct from being due to whatever disease, such as diabetes, is causing their kidney failure, or from any other unrelated diseases or, indeed, attributed correctly or not to 'getting old') is variable, but one would not automatically assume kidney disease to be the cause of symptoms when the function is above 20 per cent, and dialysis would often not be needed until kidney function had declined to around 10 per cent. Renal medicine is unusual not only in that we have effective treatments to replace the complete loss of an organ system, but also that that organ can decline to such an advanced state before those treatments 'need' to be invoked. (The reason for the inverted commas will become apparent later.)

There are several points here, but two are of particular note. The first is that many patients will have advanced kidney disease without being aware of it. This has a large impact on how they are treated and, in particular, some of the choices that have a major effect on their lives, as well as on their health. As many as one third of patients starting dialysis will only have attended a renal clinic for the first time within the preceding three months, despite having had renal disease for years. The other point, for patients attending a renal clinic from an earlier stage, is that discussions about their future treatment can be difficult, not least because of a sense of unreality or even denial. On the one hand, it is right for patients to be fully involved in decision-making: it respects autonomy however that is considered. Engagement is known to lead to better outcomes; it is what many patients want, and it usually leads to better and more effective management. In the context of the 'how do you help patients realise their life's meaning?', this is the keystone. But there is a problem: doing that early, at around, say, 20–25 per cent of kidney function, means talking about life-changing decisions at a time well before they are needed and, more challengingly for the patient, at a time when the patient may not really perceive themselves to be that ill, and understandably so if they are holding down a full-time job. The fact that kidney function is likely to decline to the point where treatments such as dialysis are needed, but that we often cannot predict when, complicates this.

What are the treatment options for patients with advanced kidney disease? I concentrate here on treatments for kidney failure, that is, the loss of most or all of kidney function *per se*, regardless of its cause, and ignore any treatments for specific causes of kidney disease or for some of the complications such as high blood pressure. This is partly for simplicity, partly because it is of most relevance to our subject and partly because there comes a stage where the emphasis is exactly that: how to manage with limited or no kidney function, regardless of underlying cause.

Broadly speaking, we can divide the options into three: transplantation, dialysis of different forms, and undertaking neither. The last option is something that in our unit we refer to as 'maximum conservative care' (MCC), the 'conservative' indicating that dialysis is not part of the treatment, the 'maximum' indicating active treatment short of that is still in place. This is in contrast to palliative care that focuses on the last stages of life in someone who is dying. Other terms are used for the same concept elsewhere. These are obviously different in what they involve, but are also different at a more fundamental level.

The decision between transplant and dialysis is not purely a preference-based choice, and nor are these two treatments alternatives. Generally, dialysis is available when needed, even if there may be limitations on the exact form, and very few patients would be unable to undertake it. On the other hand, many patients will never be fit enough to receive a transplant, as kidney disease is often a complication of other illnesses and commoner in older patients who may also have unrelated problems which preclude transplants, or will have periods when they cannot have transplants. Also, unless a patient has someone prepared to donate a kidney, it is unlikely they will have a transplant before they need dialysis. They will join a waiting list for a kidney from a deceased donor with an average waiting time of around three years. Thus, for some patients, a transplant is, for medical reasons, not a possibility, and for others, a preference, but not an alternative to dialysis, in that they will need dialysis before a transplant can be offered.

Transplants, providing there are no complications, offer the best combination of quality of life (near normal) and duration of life for those who can have them. Even for those patients, they are frequently not available at the point when a patient's own kidneys are no longer adequate. For these reasons, but particularly because life with a good quality transplant is close to a normal healthy life, transplantation effectively resolves the issue of how we manage disease while also supporting 'the soul' or the patient's aspirations for their life and what makes meaning for it. I will say little else about transplantation. I will, however, note that by not merely offering transplantation as an option but actively supporting it, as individuals and as a unit, we are supporting the minimisation of disruption of life that kidney disease and its treatment can cause. At the risk of straying from the topic and from my personal direct practice for those people who donate kidneys via our unit, including so-called 'altruistic donors', my colleagues may even help people find a new meaning.

Dialysis can have many descriptions. It is life-saving, although for the very old or very frail, that is not certain. It provides a reasonable quality of life, and we would expect dialysis patients of working age to be at work but, even when the quality of life does not appear great, for many patients the alternative of a reduced 'quantity of life', that is, death, is not an acceptable alternative. Dialysis is intrusive and time-consuming. Being on dialysis is not the same as having a well-functioning kidney, (whether that is your own healthy kidney or a transplant).

Dialysis is the mainstay of treatment for advanced kidney disease. There are few patients who cannot undertake it, at least initially, and at least in some forms, and it is able to be used when needed. For some patients, it will be something they start when their kidney disease has advanced to a certain point and which they then remain on until their death. For others, it is something they do until a transplant becomes available. Transplants don't last forever, and some patients will move to dialysis when a transplant fails. The issues are about how dialysis is done, what it involves and what else is involved. Some of these decisions take some patients a long time to make and, depending on choice, there may then be a greater or lesser amount of preparation. Some of that requires thinking and acting months ahead of a time that cannot be clearly identified, actions that can only take place when the patient has come to a firm decision. Ideally, this is completed before dialysis is needed if patients are going to have the full range of choice that good quality care involves, not least to minimise the effect of treatment on the patient's ability to fulfil their life as best they can. This is the reason for starting discussions early, albeit with the risk to which I alluded above, namely, that for some patients that may be too early.

For a patient considering dialysis I think there are two basic questions. The first is where they are going to have dialysis, which to some extent is a question of whether they are able, with the support of their partner or family, to undertake their own treatment and are willing to do so. The second is what form of dialysis they are going to undertake: haemodialysis (HD) or peritoneal dialysis (PD). HD is essentially an intermittent treatment: if done in hospital or a satellite unit, it involves typically four hours of treatment, not counting travelling or waiting, thrice weekly; if done at home, the same regime can be followed, although many patients will do the same weekly time but as more sessions that are shorter sessions, and patients are then spared the travelling and waiting time. PD is often a continuous treatment with the patient undertaking a procedure lasting around 30 minutes, four times a day. Another version of it takes place overnight every night. HD can be done at home or hospital. PD is intended to be a home-based treatment. PD (one form at least) requires a patient to do something several times every day but is more portable: a patient can take all that is needed to work or away for a few days. HD leaves a patient free of any dialysis four days a week but, if done in hospital or a satellite unit, dominates the other three days. Most units work to capacity with little flexibility, with booked sessions not necessarily at the time the patient prefers. Arranging dialysis away from the patient's unit, if they wish to travel, is not always easy.

I could have started by saying HD is a high technology technique purifying the blood directly, whereas PD is a lower technology technique using the abdominal cavity membranes to purify the blood. PD is easier for patients to learn to do themselves and may also be more feasible in some forms of accommodation. I could also have started by talking about the different forms of surgery patients need to prepare them for the different techniques.

I didn't, because this may be one of the ways in which I support minimising the impact of treatment on life. My emphasis in discussing this with patients is not, initially at least, on technique (and actually, our dialysis nurses who perform these techniques and train patients to do so will provide more practical explanations than I might) but on impact of treatments on their life. As a trainee, I remember seeing two patients whose lives were transformed by changing the type of dialysis they did, but those changes were in opposite directions. One patient moved from PD to HD; she then had Sundays free for her religious observances that were lengthy and involved travelling. Attending hospital thrice weekly was a mere inconvenience compared with missing church. For another patient, the convenience of moving from hospital HD to home PD (for him, home HD was not practical), giving him more hour-by-hour flexibility and avoiding time-consuming travel to hospital thrice weekly, was equally transforming.

This is not to say that the other aspects, including the purely technical ones, are not relevant. They are vitally so, both to the dialysis working effectively, especially if the patient is doing it themselves, and to the patient's choice. For some patients, they may be paramount. For instance, there is a patient who would consider dialysis at home but whose spouse, who would have to have some involvement, if only to deal with any problems, is too squeamish to cope with any home-based treatment.

My feeling, however, is that it is how the parts of life that are not 'treatment times' are affected, which is, for many patients, critical. I could cite a number of patients who say things like, 'I can do anything provided it doesn't interfere with my Wednesday evening bridge night,' so we are looking at hospital HD on a Tuesday/Thursday/Saturday schedule; or, 'We like to go away in the campervan every weekend,' hospital HD Monday/Wednesday/Friday or maybe PD; 'Sorry, but it's long weekends;

sometimes we go including Friday or Monday or both,' looking more like PD, and the campervan will be big enough to take sufficient amounts of the fluids used.

Of course, we do have to be happy that these treatment options are all medically appropriate for that patient, which usually they will be. For treatments that are hard to follow – and a dialysis patient has stringent limits on diet, fluid and other aspects of their life that are less 'negotiable' in terms of their health, especially if the patient is doing it at home, taking more responsibility and possibly affecting the family in unanticipated ways – there has to be 'buy-in' from the patient. Sometimes this means agreeing to a treatment choice that is unlikely to be successful, providing it is not likely to be dangerous, that a patient makes so that they have had their choice respected and can then accept the less desirable but more effective treatment at a later date.

Neither are the dialysis choices irrevocable. As my anecdotes about the two patients changing types of dialysis indicate, people can move between them. Sometimes moves are forced by medical reasons, 'technical failures' and so on. For some patients, choice is dictated by reasons neither we nor they can control. A patient who had recently started hospital HD then asked about home HD; I was surprised that that had not been considered before. It seems that the patient had identified practical problems which they felt were too difficult to resolve and that the patient felt hospital HD would be easier. After a few weeks of travelling and having to fit into the then available slots, the patient reconsidered these problems and felt they might be surmountable. With further exploration it turned out that some of these problems may be real barriers to home therapy which are beyond our or the patient's control (rented accommodation and the landlord not allowing the necessary modifications). It may be that we do achieve what the patient wants, but I think even if we can't, we will at least have demonstrated that what we are doing is trying to minimise the impact of treatment so far as we are able. We may find that the barriers are insurmountable, but we haven't simply assumed that, and, as far as we can, we have optimised the patient's ability to live their life to the best their best.

Then there is the option of maximum conservative care (MCC). We continue to see patients, treat such complications of advanced kidney disease as are amenable to drug treatment, manage symptoms and so on, but do not move on to dialysis at a time when the kidney function would otherwise merit it. The acceptance is that the patient could die of renal failure that dialysis could have prevented. That is our acceptance, and it should be that of the patient and their relatives, although there are some last-minute changes of mind that are not always successful. These are difficult areas for some patients to understand, and even more so for them to accept and apply to themselves. They may be surprised when we admit what we can't predict.

The majority of patients who opt for MCC are elderly or frail, or usually both. We do dialyse elderly patients and not just those who have grown old on dialysis. There aren't many people who opt for dialysis when they are over 90, but it's not unknown. I make that point just to clarify that while patients opting for MCC are largely elderly, that is because it is their choice, not ours. I would have to acknowledge that we are likely, if only subconsciously, to have some influence on their choice, but there is not a basic assumption of 'too old for dialysis'. With age comes frailty and multiple illnesses, and these have two effects. They may be what someone on MCC dies from. Thus, while we accept that a patient on MCC may die of renal failure, that is not inevitably the case; death may come in another form. The second point is that dialysis is not a trivial undertaking and it, coupled with the other aspects of treatment on dialysis (dietary restrictions and so on), may just be too much, either beyond the patient's physical abilities to tolerate, or beyond what is acceptable for them. Recognising that, and that death is inevitable, I would take as part of this topic of 'the soul', the raison d'être, or perhaps the reason no longer 'to be', at least as a living person.

The issue for the elderly and frail with advanced kidney disease is that first, we can't predict their life span, nor anyone else's, but when you are close to natural death and are discussing treatments for one component of your health you do consider that. Second, we can't predict how well they will cope with or respond to dialysis with any precision.

Hence we can't tell by how much or even whether dialysis will prolong their life. Of course, it's not all about quantity of life, certainly not in the context of this chapter, but we do know something about quality: not so much about absolute quality of life, if such a thing exists, but about how it changes. In general, my experience is that a frail patient will not do much on a dialysis day other than dialyse; that and travelling is hard work, and they may not be up to doing anything else. The trajectory of dying with untreated renal failure is a reasonably stable quality of life, whatever that may be in absolute terms, and symptoms are controllable with medication. Taking these together, then, at a rough approximation, to get the same number of useful days at home – that is, days when life is lived rather than just existed, the days when life has a meaning – dialysis would have to prolong life twofold. We can't tell that for an individual, and currently we can't be certain, for some groups of patients, that it ever does.

It is therefore entirely reasonable – and I think life-affirming, as distinct from supporting existence – to discuss this frankly with the patient, and a number decline to consider dialysis. As I sometimes express it, 'The question for you is whether you want as little contact with hospital as possible, but closing the opportunity that we might prolong your life, or to live as long as possible but spending around half of what's left to you coming to hospital.' Some patients value the former, some the latter, some have a life event they want to aim for, will dialyse for a while, and may then withdraw. These are discussions that sometimes take a long time.

My reason for putting 'need' in inverted commas may now be clear. For some people, dialysis will be the wrong decision and a path not taken. In some situations, although a treatment such as dialysis is available and would work technically, it is not needed in the sense that treatment may not be needed. A natural and non-technological death may be exactly that: natural. In these situations, dialysis is 'needed' in the sense that it is the way to prolong life if that is desired, assuming, of course, that it does, which is not always the case, but it is not needed in the sense that life must always be prolonged, not 'preserved' at all costs. 'Need' can be a difficult word.

I haven't considered withdrawal from dialysis, which is a related but distinct topic. In terms of withdrawing, with the expectation of death shortly afterwards, although 'shortly' may be three or four weeks, the life-affirming aspect, I think, is really in the self-determination it represents. People withdrawing from dialysis are not doing so in order to start some new project, in this life at least.

I have also restricted this to patients who have mental capacity; to discuss the implications of lacking that in this context would require more space than is available.

Summarising my response to the request, 'Describe how you manage patients medically in a way that supports them spiritually, that is to say, allows them to give meaning to their life,' in the context of patients with advanced kidney disease, I would say the following:

1. Autonomy, while being a problematic concept, is of some relevance and, respecting that, enabling patients to make their own choices plays into the 'living their life to their best'.
2. In practical terms, treatments for advanced kidney disease are intrusive and time-consuming; hence supporting patients to optimise their lives means giving them as wide a choice of appropriate treatments as possible. None is perfect, none suits every patient.
3. That means having the full range of treatments available at all times rather than constraining patients' choices. That is a challenge for the service and supporting system not addressed by the individual doctor when in clinic with their patient, requiring considerable resources, both material and in a range of staff. We are fortunate in that respect.
4. As a doctor, one has to understand those treatments and the effects they have, not so much medical as social (time involved, etc.). Other members of the multi-professional team are key to

this, and a final decision may well be made with one of our nurse specialists.

5. The patient has to consider, and be adequately informed to consider, how those effects play out in their life. We have to accept we will not automatically know what is best, although we may well recognise in some cases that some options are not viable. Some patients will want the clinical team to be more actively involved in making a decision.

6. This may all take a long time, including a long time in clinic. Patients need that support and encouragement.

When I started to prepare this, I had planned to centre it on a few patients in detail, and made notes of relevant discussions in clinic. To enhance confidentiality, I then decided to mix them into some more generic hypothetical patients, but still with a narrative base. What I have ended up doing is largely to describe a process, albeit patient-centred, with a few brief and focused examples of specific points. Maybe I am closer to the 'process' part of the scale, the existence of which I dispute! I think I have actually described an approach.

I have not referenced this. Basic principles of medical practice are readily available from websites such as that of the General Medical Council (GMC), and the patient-centred part of me wrote this without referring to any texts. Those interested in some of the more specialised guidance and information about prevalence of dialysis, survival and so on might look at the websites of the Renal Association and the related organisation, the UK Renal Registry.

10

Stroke

THE HEART OF THE MATTER

Nicola Gainsborough

Dr Nicola Gainsborough, MB ChB, FRCP, is a consultant stroke physician and, as Honorary Senior Clinical Lecturer, is Phase 3 Lead for Brighton and Sussex Medical School.

The Stroke Unit

We work in a medium-sized multidisciplinary stroke unit with 23 beds in the oldest part of the hospital, built in 1826, on the third floor, approached by a steep staircase with a deep brown smooth banister or equally ancient and temperamental lifts.

The ward is split into two sections separated by a very narrow corridor, off which sits the day room and the cupboard that functions as a clinic for up to five patients and their relatives. Alongside this is a small gym area that used to be a bed space for three beds until we nailed the plinths down, so they couldn't be moved. Technically there are two teams of nurses that run of each side of the ward, but there is a constant flow of life between the sections: borrowing the hoist; finding the shampoo; providing help from the HCAs (healthcare assistants) when one side is very busy; therapists treating patients and bringing them into the gym; ushering relatives through to find their family member just arrived up from A&E; sitting clinic patients in the day room for their appointments;

moving patients around to make another bed space for a sick patient who requires closer observation and care.

It is therefore unusual for the ward to be still and we are certainly not smart, modern or slick when first observed. It is in this space we care for stroke patients of all ages, all faiths and all physical and mental conditions, and for whom we try to make this the best experience we can, be it on the pathway home or as part of the final stage of the patient's life.

The staff are key to our care, and many have been on the unit since our inception over 12 years ago. We are a mixed group: funny, quiet, light-touch, chatty, serious, emotional, Filipino, Polish, Icelandic, Brazilian, Russian, Brightonian, Latvian, Irish, Italian, gay, straight, transgender, noisy, religious, atheist, and each of us with our own innate spirituality, accepting of all. There is a sense of family here and a community bound by friendship, consideration, kindness and a willingness to do whatever it takes to care for our patients, often without being asked. The structure is as flat as it can be, and the ward manager runs the unit with commitment, a light touch and an easy sense of humour. All the staff, regardless of their actual role, can and do turn their hand to anything required for the patients. We also receive valuable help from other teams: social workers, mental health, palliative care, oncology, surgery, therapists, pharmacists, actors, the chaplaincy team, singers, volunteers, kitchen staff, cleaners, readers, porters and radiographers, to mention just a few who make the unit hum.

The patient and the patient's family

In and around this unit, activity is centred on the patient. Finding the patient at the heart is what really matters. I am not sure any of us would label what we do to find this as 'spiritual', but this is, in essence, what we are trying to discover. Having a stroke, for the majority of patients and their families, can be seen as a time of great change, and is often associated with a huge sense of loss and fear. There can be loss of speech and motor function, loss of cognitive faculties, loss of control and independence of role and a sense of sadness, all in parallel to an often profound and prolonged fatigue around the time of a stroke. To get to the core, or even part of it, for a patient takes time and is not something achieved on the first day of admission.

Acute stroke care today is an urgent and time-critical, often initially requiring rapid assessments, immediate head scanning, potent drugs delivered intravenously and sometimes more complex and lengthy treatments in the laboratory with the neuroradiology team. This beginning of the patient's care occurs in the Emergency Department, often in a noisy and busy resuscitation bay, then through to CT scanning, into the laboratory and then the journey to the ward via three lifts, a long underground corridor, a bumpy and windy outside tunnel, to finally arrive on the unit. These first hours are often fast paced and can involve up to 12 members of staff, trying to salvage as much brain as possible and to minimise future disability. This requires concentration, analysis, attention to detail, with little time for social niceties. During an acute stroke the patient loses up to two million neurons per minute, so every minute matters.

The journey to the unit, however, is often the first time we have to be alone with the patient and their family, away from the initial drama of their arrival in the Emergency Department. The often long wait for the lifts and equally long corridors provide an important time to start to break the ice, to begin to get to know the patient and their family. It helps to be able to reassure, to allay fears and anxieties in opening up these conversations, and often we learn much in this initial hour.

The safe arrival on the ward for the patient and the team is a moment to take a breath, to get the patient quietly and calmly settled into the bed or chair, sort out the monitoring equipment, welcome the relatives and find them some space in the day room with some NHS tea. Sometimes, difficult and painful conversations have to happen almost immediately if the patients are very sick and at a time when we know next to nothing of our patients or their families.

On a better day, the picture starts with the basics taken on admission about next of kin, neighbours, carers and who to call in an emergency. Often this provides useful information about the patient's network and what roots them in the family and community in which they live. On occasion, there can be no one. General practitioners, district nurses and social workers in these circumstances can often provide vital information about the patient's health, life and wishes.

More details are gathered by the therapists, nurses and unit staff as they treat the patients. What do they enjoy, what are the patient's goals for a good life, what food do they like, what sport or films do they like to watch, which football team do they support, what and who is it that really matters to them, and what would help to get them home from hospital? Being with the patient 24 hours a day provides the space and time to have these conversations. None of the conversations is formulaic or standard, and frequently it takes time to build up an understanding and a picture of life before the stroke and how the patient, their family and friends envisage life afterwards.

Conversations with families happen frequently and with many members of staff: by phone early in the morning or late at night; face-to-face on the ward; in the gym as part of rehabilitation sessions; during mealtimes when families may come in to help to feed their relative; as part of formal planning meetings; and via email and letter. These all build on the information we already have, particularly contributing details of previous conversations about influences, in what way or how the patient would wish to live, their previous mood, thoughts on religion, spirituality, death, dying and resuscitation. Some of these conversations uncover family sadness and loss, misunderstandings, disagreements, schisms and long periods of impasse and separation that contribute to our understanding of the complicated lives of each of our patients.

Care of the dying

Stroke is not always a survivable disease, and we care for over a hundred dying patients every year. Care of the dying is an important part of the practice of good medicine. We only have one go to get this particular time in our patients' lives right, and often few options to make things better after a patient has died. The dying process itself, for families and staff, can often feel hard and in some ways as physically and emotionally effortful as delivery and birth without the hullabaloo surrounding it, but it is an equally important rite of passage for those departing and those left behind. Understanding our patients and their families during this process is critical to ensuring the best care. Asking directly about spiritual needs or religious faith kindly, compassionately and with an open mind is important. Usually these conversations occur away from the patient. A quiet place, adequately cleared and with a door that can be closed, is ideal but not always possible. Allowing families and friends time to reflect on these conversations is important, where possible, as many families have never had such discussions and find this particularly difficult. We always try to ask if the patient is religious and if they would find it comforting to have a prayer said, or for a rabbi, imam or priest to attend. Some say yes and we arrange for the relevant minister or chaplain to attend, or the family may organise this themselves. Other families are adamant that their relative would not want this, but find other ways to mark the passing of their life.

One family, whose father died in December, wanted softer lights than the NHS could provide, and strung up fairy lights in the shape of a Christmas tree in his room. During the following days there was always someone with him, young grandchildren passing through, sometimes silent, sometimes talking, and the room had a calm and happy atmosphere throughout this period. It took us many months to take these lights down. Another family of a much younger patient dying of a brain tumour personalised his whole bed space within the ward for him, with photographs, cards, plants, coloured blankets, music; it was grotto-like for his last few days, but it was his, and their, sacred space for that time.

Returning from my own mother's death at home, and time around her bed with our family, made me aware of how little experience relatives may have of death and dying, and how frightening this may be. It is important that staff spend time with families to talk through what might happen, how the patient's breathing can change, what that means, what care can be given and how, and that for the majority of patients the actual moment of death is usually calm and dignified and occurs during sleep. Some families need to talk after the patient has died. One family in particular needed time to talk in the room immediately after their mother had died about their frustrations and fears during her last few months. This felt an important conversation to be had there and then, and happened around the patient's bed soon after her death.

Compiling information for us all to understand and respect

Most of the information we collect is recorded in a booklet for each patient, set up by our speech therapist initially, for those patients who are unable to speak following their stroke, but now used for all our patients. We ask the patient, their family and friends to complete what they can and leave it in the bedside folder to add to, as and when they wish. The booklet has developed over the years and is regularly reviewed and contributed to by the team. It provides the central source of information alongside the patient's clinical and discharge notes that record the conversations with families. A copy of the booklet is to be found at the end of this chapter for reference.

We meet as a team three times a week to review the patient's progress and to begin to plan for their discharge from our care. This provides a valuable space and confidential time for sharing, and we are able to assimilate all this information to provide a clearer, holistic picture of the patient and the family we are caring for and treating. It also ensures a consistency and shared understanding of the needs of individual patients. Most patients remain on the unit for between 9 and 13 days, with some stays considerably shorter or longer.

We also run bi-monthly afternoon meetings over tea, where we invite our patients, families and carers back to see us, away from the ward, to share their experience of the unit, of being discharged home, of ongoing therapy, care and follow-up. It is an important time to learn where things didn't go so well, gaps or failings in our provision, and what new things we can try in order to improve our patient care. We learn much from these meetings and they provide important drivers for changes for our service. We invite a patient each year to be part of our unit governance meetings, and their contributions and input into changes for patients from this group are invaluable.

For staff

Providing exemplary care in the NHS is not always easy and requires commitment, a shared vision and ethos, early starts, late finishes, flexibility, stamina and a sense of humour, alongside a willingness to push the system as hard as you can, to get the best for your patients. The vast majority of our team will turn their hand to most jobs on the unit with good grace and without being asked. This type of care can come at a price for staff, with burnout, sickness and high staff turnover on many units today. We are extremely fortunate to have a stable workforce, with at least five of our original staff still working with us 12 years after setting up the unit. Our staff sickness rates are low, and others are keen to work with us. Having a shared vision and commitment is critical, as is the importance of balancing the work we do with our families and social lives. Together we eat a lot of cake. We go to the pub, football and rugby, have ward tea parties at the drop of a hat with some very competitive team baking, and carols at Christmas with more cake. We laugh together and look out for each other much of the time. Exercise, cycling, the gym, quiet space, gardening, time with our families and friends, prayer, time out and booking holidays all help. We say thank you a lot and mean it.

More recently we have set up regular monthly meetings specifically for staff on the acute and rehabilitation units, where we take an hour out to talk together and reflect on the care of a patient or their family that may have been particularly challenging. We bring cake and set up the meeting in a safe and confidential manner, with the door closed, so staff feel comfortable about expressing their uncertainties, vulnerability and fears. The care of complex patients is rarely black and white, and at times we may be uncertain about what is the right thing to do. Sharing this helps. We are none of us perfect. Ideas spring from these meetings; some we follow and others not, but it allows us some specific time to reflect and support one another in our work together.

Why does it matter?

Without understanding your patient and what makes life worth living for them is like treating half a patient. The medicine and nursing are often straightforward, but finding and contributing to the most holistic recovery involves more than these superficial basics. Knowing that the patient's two sons died of a fatal, genetically inherited disease contributes to his anger, frustration, sadness, low mood, abuse of alcohol and recreational drugs and the need to lash out in hospital following his stroke. The academic whose mother died of stroke disease and vascular dementia, whose every conversation with us about his own disease is angry and aggressive, with no initial acknowledgment of his fears of a similar fate until he articulated this and we understood these facts. The face of the patient when his tiny dog came to the ward with his neighbours, knowing the dog was fine, gave him the reassurance that all was okay at home when our words had not.

Knowing what really matters and lies at the core for patients and their families allows us to adapt our care for each individual, be it the bed space, the food, the music, the rabbi or orthodox priest attending, the soft blankets that comfort, the dog beside the bed, the phone call at the desk to the son in Australia or the fairy lights to stave off the passing night.

**Brighton and Sussex
University Hospitals**
NHS Trust

From the RSCH Stoke Team

We would like to know more about your relative/friend to help us get to know them, communicate as effectively as possible and ensure their care is tailored to their needs. We would be pleased if you could let us know more about him/her.

Please feel free to complete as much or as little of this form as you wish. This information may also be used to set therapy goals in the future.

Thank you very much.

Name of the person this form is about: _____

How would he/she like to be addressed by hospital staff? _____

Does anyone live with the person? If so, who?

_____

Marital status: single ☐   married ☐ (approx. number of years? _____)
divorced ☐   widowed ☐ (how long ago? _____)
Name of spouse: _____

HEALTH (before the stroke)
Eyesight/glasses? _____

Hearing aids worn? _____

Dentures worn? _____

Mobile? Yes/No   Mobility aids? Indoors _____ Outdoors _____
Stairs? Yes/No   Access steps? Yes/No   Rails on stair/steps _____

Any history of falls? _____

Are you aware of any difficulties/issues the person was having at home (before the stroke)? _____

_____

Care at home? Yes/No   How many times a day? _____

Provider of care? _____

Pets: If the person has any pets, please let us know their names, etc.:

_____

FAMILY (please include nicknames)

Name	Relationship	Where they live	Regular contact?
_____			Yes/No
_____			Yes/No
_____			Yes/No
_____			Yes/No
_____			Yes/No
_____			Yes/No

FRIENDS

Name   Details (e.g. how they are known, for how long, etc.)

_____

_____

_____

_____

LIFE INFORMATION

Personality and interests

How would you describe your friend/relative's personality before the stroke? This information will help us interact with your friend/relative in a way that will make them feel comfortable.

_____

_____

_____

Where has the person lived? _____

_____

What have been his/her important life activities? (e.g. jobs, family or voluntary responsibilities) _____

_____

_____

_____

Which languages does he/she speak? _____

Does the person have strong religious or political beliefs?

_____

_____

How did the person spend an average day before the stroke?

_____

_____

_____

Television: Which programmes does the person particularly enjoy?

_____

_____

Radio: Which station/programmes does the person listen to?

_____

_____

Hobbies: (e.g. gardening, sewing, cooking, films, sports, DIY)

_____

_____

Sports: Is the person interested in, or do they play, any sports?
If so, which teams, etc.?

_____

_____

Music: Is the person interested in any particular kinds of music?

_____

_____

_____

Reading: If the person enjoyed reading, what type of books, papers, magazines?

_____

_____

_____

Were there any difficulties with writing before the stroke? Yes ☐   No ☐

Are there any places that hold fond memories for the person?
(e.g. favourite holidays)

_____

_____

Can you think of any topics that ought to be avoided because of their painful
association for the patient?

_____

_____

FOOD AND DRINK
While it is difficult for your friend/relative to tell us, please let us know
whether he/she would be likely to drink the following?

(strong/weak? milk/sugar?)

Tea _____

Coffee _____

Hot chocolate _____

Does the person have any special dietary needs?
Diabetic ☐   Vegetarian ☐   Vegan ☐   Halal ☐   Kosher ☐
Other (please specify): _____

Are there any foods which the person tends not to eat or that they
particularly enjoy?

_____

_____

_____

_____

Your name (person filling out form): _____

What is your relationship with the person? _____

Please leave your telephone number, if we may contact you: _____

Date form filled in: _____

Thank you for your help.

*****

If you can think of any more information that may be helpful, please feel free
to add it below.

_____

_____

_____

_____

_____

_____

_____

_____

_____

_____

11

Palliative Care in the Community

LOOKING IN 'HIDDEN PLACES' – ASSESSING SPIRITUAL PAIN AND DISTRESS

Rachel Reed and Nigel Spencer

Rachel Reed, BSc (Hons), graduated in Psychology with Nursing Studies from City University and St Bartholomew's Hospital, London. Rachel has worked within the speciality of palliative care in various roles, including: managing the implementation of the Liverpool Care Pathway in Brighton and Hove, and as a Macmillan clinical nurse specialist. She has worked most recently as a lecturer in palliative care at St Barnabas House, Worthing. Rachel is a mindfulness practitioner.

Nigel Spencer, BSc (Hons), qualified from Middlesex University in 1999 as a registered general nurse. He specialised in cancer nursing, obtaining a BSc (Hons) from King's College London. Nigel works as a community palliative care nurse practitioner at St Catherine's Hospice in Crawley. Nigel has a keen interest in teaching. He has previously run groups on self-esteem and purposefulness, empowering people to achieve living to their own individual potential. In 2013 Nigel became a Dementia Friends Champion.

A conversation between two nursing colleagues, Rachel Reed (RR) and Nigel Spencer (NS)

WHERE DO WE BEGIN?

RR: What helps you do a spiritual assessment? A tool or format? What questions do you ask?

NS: I approach a spiritual assessment as part of a conversation. It's about facilitating direction, it's listening to patients and extrapolating some kind of focus, helping patients to see the meaning they're putting on their illness and the associated struggle. It needs to be more natural than a tick-box exercise. If I stop and think about what I am setting out to achieve when doing a spiritual care assessment, I want patients to feel that they are important. It's remembering the little things that make them different as a person. It's about bringing out the best in them and making them feel special. It's about reminding them of who they are without the distress, pain, neediness, dependence. It's about entering into a relationship where patients and nurses let go of their roles and are free to be two individuals enjoying a human connection. This is true 'communion', celebrating who each person is.

The value of having a model is that it gives some structure to what you're trying to achieve. There are many models and assessment tools that can help to link up the content of the conversation into a format that is easier to work with. Assessment tools can help to quantify and illuminate the amount of struggle and distress that the patient is experiencing.

RR: But the skill, presumably, is using that flexibly so that it doesn't come across as an interview technique, or that you're just asking specific questions. You would allow the conversation to flow. What about if people don't want to talk about it? As sometimes they don't.

NS: I see it as being able to plant that seed so that the conversation is available to them if and when the patient wants to or is ready to have it. Waiting for them to have a deeper or more specific conversation about faith and beliefs in their own time or bringing it up in a general nursing assessment or a symptom review for something like pain or anxiety. Patients often say they don't want to talk about it, but not many patients say don't ever mention that to me again. I think it is a conversation which, as the relationship and trust develops, can be built on and deepened as we get to different places, both the practitioner and the patient, during the disease trajectory. As the illness progresses towards death, priorities often change and the struggles can intensify as patients experience their time running out. This is often when fears increase: fear of the unknown, fear of leaving behind relatives that they may have been responsible for, fear of not having reconciled regrets, events or relationships in their past, fear of death.

RR: That's a big part of what makes people's lives matter.

NS: Yes, absolutely. It is often in addressing the more immediate symptom issues and gaining patients' trust that conversations can then lead to the more existential concerns. What I mean by existential concerns is suffering that is not relieved by treatment of physical symptoms (Hospice and Palliative Nurses Association no date). Some possible causes of existential distress could be:

- the idea of death itself
- fear or discomfort around a particular health crisis near death
- loss of will to live
- loss of meaning or purpose in life
- profound loneliness, intolerable emptiness, sadness
- alienation, loss of a sense of dignity.

By helping patients to recognise this through providing a safe space to explore and acknowledge their increasing levels of stress and anxiety, we can reassure patients that they are not alone and that it is natural to have these difficult feelings when experiencing a terminal illness. It is honouring 'what is'. We can then work out how we can support them with 'being with' these difficulties if they want support.

RR: I have often thought that our role is to start those conversations that people may find hard to have with their loved ones.

NS: Rachel, you say they are hard conversations to have. Yes, I agree with you, that most times they are. We, as healthcare practitioners, have a responsibility to give patients the space and choice to have these conversations. They are often avoided for understandable reasons, but this is not helpful and supportive for the patients, and does need to be challenged. The question that I am often left with is, who is fearful of having these conversations? Often I see the fear in patients and families, but also in our colleagues, both nurses and GPs.

RR: I think it would be good to explore why you think colleagues find these conversations hard to have. I know that when we discuss this in the classroom, nurses often feel unsure and ill equipped to have conversations they perceive as 'difficult', feeling they do not have the time, or won't know what to say, or that they fear opening a can of worms.

NS: I see it as an opportunity to enter into the messiness of life (and death and dying). Together we need to acknowledge their messiness without judgement, in order for us to start to work with it, to talk about the difficulties and struggles. It is in the messiness that we help patients find some of the reasons and previous life experiences that may be causing the feelings of increased fear and discomfort. It is when we help patients find, articulate and express those things they are struggling with, that we can formulate a care plan with the aim to reduce and sometimes alleviate the distress, the fear, the discomfort, the pain.

WHAT DO WE MEAN BY PAIN?
NS: So if we use the analogy of physical pain as a lead-in to our conversation specifically about spiritual pain or distress. Patients will often mask the pain. Why do patients mask pain? I think there is often fear. If they acknowledge the pain, then what often follows is the thinking that the disease must be worse, the tumour bigger, my illness is progressing! Masking the pain in the beginning stages of a deterioration in health helps to maintain a sense of control. (A sense of control can start to slip away in a lot of areas of daily living with the increasing impact of symptoms on independence, such as increasing weakness and tiredness, and decreasing mobility.) Seeing someone you love or care for in pain often causes emotional pain and psychological discomfort in itself, so the natural response is towards protection. Patients protecting

their loved ones and family, and loved ones protecting the patient by not acknowledging what they may be feeling, seeing or observing. Denial is a very useful coping strategy that allows patients or family members and/or both to deal with the volume of distress that they are able to tolerate at their own pace. The downside of denial is collusion and the risk of letting difficulties escalate to a point of crisis where decisions need to be made in a hurry and are more distressing. The picture of a pressure cooker comes to mind where an explosion can result if it is left too long, not releasing the pressure that is building up.

RR: Often denial can be very protective. If it's too painful for people to bear then they won't go there. You have to allow that to be okay.

NS: Yes, to a certain degree, but we also need to keep our eye on the levels of increasing discomfort and pain (pressure) and try to find ways of easing the pain (letting out some steam). So it is often about balancing protection and collusion against action and gentle confrontation. There is also the flip side whereby not acknowledging the pain of the situation, you're not able to talk about it, thus making it more difficult to deal with and support patients and families.

RR: As palliative care practitioners, we have a historical foundation based on Dame Cicely Saunders' work and the concept of 'total pain', where she talks about the holistic nature of pain and how emotional, psychosocial and spiritual distress affect the physical pain. In order to help and support patients with total pain, we need to help them identify all aspects that are having an impact. We are talking to patients and finding out what has been happening, to create a picture for the patient to see. Once we are able to see the picture together, we can start to try and improve the parts that are problematic.

NS: Dass and Gorman (1985) have a very helpful description of what we're talking about here, in the chapter on 'Helping Prison', in their book *How Can I Help?* They explore how our roles can entrap us. The way

I make sense of some of this is to imagine a picture where there is our patient living with the terminal illness and moving along the disease trajectory. In parallel, there are the family and friends going along the same trajectory, supporting the patient and living through similar trials and difficulties with a different perspective and often experiencing some similar emotions. The temptation for both patient and family members often is to close down and try to deal with it in their own ways to protect each other. Communication becomes difficult and doesn't flow. The aim here is for the family to protect the patient and the patient to protect the family. The outcome that results is that the patient and family are in parallel, but are not actually talking or communicating. I think our role, particularly in palliative care, is to bridge that gap between the parallel processes described here. We can do this by helping them to articulate what the distress, pain, struggles are. When the distress is named, it can be dealt with. It can be looked at, described, assessed, quantified and some of the unknowns can be taken away by discussing the problems. It loosens the glue that holds these tight, fearful situations together. When communication is opened up, the good aspects can be discussed and important things can be said, where expressions of love and thanks and gratitude can be offered, which in themselves are very healing. This allows patients and families to make the most of enjoying the precious time that is left before death.

WHAT GETS IN THE WAY?
RR: Let's explore why it can be so difficult to acknowledge our own struggles.

NS: Acknowledging struggle often feels uncomfortable and even painful. In my experience, patients will often prefer to use the word 'discomfort' rather than 'pain'. I think it is normal and natural for us to want to push something that is uncomfortable away. We all steer away from pain if we can. We remove the source of the discomfort or the pain. In palliative care nursing, we often cannot remove the source of the pain. This is the root of the matter. So we have to redefine a relationship. Using the symptom of pain as an example, we help patients with their relationship with the pain, by building a picture of its different parts and expressions, using descriptions of colour, texture, levels of intensity, visual descriptions like gnawing, burning, tearing. We ask them how they relate to this.

RR: Often with difficulty, as we have already mentioned. What is required is developing empathy and our ability to really hear people, listening and getting into their story.

NS: McCaffery's (1972) well-known definition, 'pain is what the patient says it is', encapsulates this for me. It is first and foremost about listening to what the patient is telling me. I try to see the picture of their pain that they are describing to me and figuratively put myself into their shoes. This is the best way for me to address someone's pain.

There are patients that I have assessed who say that they are in excruciating physical pain and there are drugs that we can give people, but there are times when some of the drugs don't actually address that pain. This is where broader assessment of other elements of pain are required: emotional, psychological and spiritual elements of the pain. These types of pain are often more complex, making them more difficult to address.

SPIRITUAL PAIN

RR: I think we now need to talk about spiritual distress or what we sometimes hear called patients' 'soul pain' (Kearney 1996). It is helpful to have a sense of what we understand by that, and a framework that can help us to explore it with patients in language that is simple and straightforward. I often find myself coming back to and using the model by Peter Kaye that I came across a long time ago now, when I was introducing and working with the Gold Standards Framework (GSF) model to improve palliative care in primary care and care homes (Thomas 2003). This simple idea suggests that often patients can have spiritual concerns about their past, present and future that can be a really helpful way to explore areas of possible spiritual distress. Thinking about their past, it is not uncommon for patients to have regrets, and sometimes guilt, often linked to their thinking about why they are now dying or have become so ill.

An example that stays with me of a patient's past impacting on their illness and dying was a man who was so guilt-ridden over an affair he had had some years ago. He was convinced that this had led to him getting cancer, from which he was now dying. He believed that his disease was his punishment for his infidelity. He had never spoken about this but had carried this guilt and conviction that he was to blame for his disease and early death, even though his affair had ended and he was fully reconciled with his wife. Remembering this and some very emotional private conversations I shared with this gentleman reminds me that I didn't have any answers. He needed to tell someone as part of processing his past life and his guilt that he still felt. I listened and let him speak, and I think the fact that I showed no judgement and allowed him the time and space to talk about it was the best thing could have done. I had worked with this gentleman and his family for many months during his treatment. I had got to know him well, and I think he had built up trust and confidence that he could talk to me. This felt a great privilege. It made me realise how important listening is and that it is all we can do, as often there are no answers. However, as I have gained more experience, I believe that people don't want, need or expect answers from us. I think if people feel heard, then they often know what they need to do. In this particular case, the patient found the courage to speak with his wife and then took up the offer to explore this further with the hospice chaplain who visited them both at home a few more times before he died. Both the patient and his wife found the visits comforting and supportive, and they helped him come to terms with his distress and difficult thoughts, which enabled him to forgive himself before dying.

Kaye (1999) talks about future concerns that can often cause spiritual distress, such as fears about the way people may die, the more existential questions that people often have about life after death, or what happens once we are dead. I remember a gentleman I nursed who was so frightened of being buried alive and people thinking he was dead when in fact he wasn't that he became terrified to fall asleep. I can still see and remember his relief once I had explained the practical procedure of verification of death and the careful checks that nurses do to be sure that a patient has actually died. Such fears need to be aired as it is only by talking about them, and giving information and discussing them, that they can be reduced.

Dame Cicely Saunders said, 'The way care is given can reach the most hidden places and give space for unexpected development' (1996, cited in Kearney 1996, p.11). So in the example I have given it was my listening that was the key to unlocking the distress, but also asking the questions and not being put off by worrying that I didn't know what to say or have all the answers. The longer I do this work, the more I come to realise that more often than not, there aren't always answers.

NS: I think that this confidence often builds with personal life experience. As nurses working in palliative care, where we are dealing with more death than the average person, it is really important not to be frightened of uncertainty and not knowing the answers. I would encourage newly qualified nurses to explore their own relationship with death and how they make sense of this important subject. This is a lifelong learning process and is evolving and is rarely neat and tidy.

RR: Back to the messiness.

NS: Yes, it is about an honesty. It's about an integrity and a compassionate professionalism. I use my life experience and the things that I have read to broaden my understanding of what I witness other people going through as they become less well. The broader this is, the more I am able to empathise and hopefully become less judgemental.

RR: I agree, all these qualities are so important. Very much how Watts and Psaila (2010) summarise how Twycross (2003) describes the important aspects of spiritual care at the end of life, as 'affirmation and acceptance of the person in a non judgemental way...open communication and a sense of "being there"...of giving time and listening' (Watts and Psaila 2010, p.128). I think it's also about allowing people to be as they are, and respecting that. Spiritual distress is such an individual thing, that every person you go and meet is different, and there's no 'one size fits all' in terms of how you go about a spiritual assessment or conversation.

HOW DO WE ASSESS SPIRITUAL NEEDS?

RR: I like this definition of spiritual care found in the Royal College of Nursing's (RCN) *Pocket Guide*, which they published after a survey they did, which identified that nurses felt they needed more guidance in how to give spiritual care. 'Spiritual care begins with encouraging human contact in a compassionate relationship and moves in whatever direction need requires' (NHS Education for Scotland 2009, cited in RCN 2011, p.3). This seems to reflect the very individual nature of spiritual needs and care.

There are so many tools and frameworks around now which can be useful and we need to be aware of them, but I do think that there is a potential risk in following them to the point that they become intrusive and like a tick-box exercise.

NS: The model I do often use is FICA (see Nurses Learning Network, nurseslearning.com). I like it because of its simplicity and the ease of remembering what the four letters stand for and the openness of the questions, as seen below.

F: What is your faith or belief?
- Do you consider yourself spiritual or religious?
- What things do you believe in that give meaning to your life?

I: Is it important in your life?
- What influence does it have on how you take care of yourself?
- How have your beliefs influenced your behaviour during this illness?
- What role do your beliefs play in regaining your health?

C: Are you part of a spiritual or religious community?
- Is this of support to you and how?
- Is there a person or group of people you really love or who are really important to you?

A: How would you like me, your healthcare provider, to address these issues in your healthcare?

RR: That is implying consent then, and partnership in assessing their spiritual needs, rather than making the assumption that we have the right as healthcare professionals to delve deep into people's past and explore areas of their lives they may consider personal and private. Some of the questions potentially could be seen as intrusive. Also, if their prognosis is poor and time is short, it is possible that there may not be enough time for people to confront deep-seated issues. This could potentially make them more distressed, or feeling forced or coerced into confronting painful issues that they may have left behind. It is so important to check whose need is being met here, the patient's or the professional's.

This links back to what you were saying about the value of denial, and reminds me of something I read recently that gave me food for thought and made me question my practice and our use of tools. Randall and Downie (2006) suggest that unthinking over-use of assessment tools could feel, to the patient, like a form of 'harassment by questioning in the name of compassion'. Unskilled or insensitive use of questions or tools could do more harm than good, especially when time is very short. If they are not seeing the same nurse and are not able to build up the trust in that relationship, then it's quite a big ask for people to perhaps disclose stuff that is very deeply personal or private. It's got to be a partnership, so what you're saying is that the FICA model asks and incorporates that, rather than assuming it is the right thing for everyone.

NS: A tool is only as good as the practitioner using it. FICA ends with a direct question about action that is needed. When we ask this question, we are giving control to the patient and it should be led by the patient. The questions from the model help us establish what the patient's problems are and opens up a conversation. Sometimes patients do not have the language to be able to express or to name some of what they are experiencing. Our role as nurses is to help them name it and put it on the table, as it were, bringing it out into the open.

RR: This is such an important point about the language we use. We need to find language that is right for the patient. This is particularly relevant if we consider the more existential aspects of spiritual distress and the questions we sometimes get asked.

NS: We do. In order to make a spiritual assessment and move situations forward for patients, we do ask quite deep, searching questions. We also get asked very difficult and challenging questions. The question I get asked the most is, 'How long have I got left?' This question has the power to open up a huge conversation, or it can be answered, often inaccurately, in one word, such as 'weeks' or maybe even 'days'. This is probably not really the question the patient is wanting answered, as the questions underneath this one are the more important ones. I think it is often best answered with another gentle question such as, 'John, what makes you ask this question?' This can open up the conversation allowing John to say, possibly for the first time, that he feels worse, or he knows he is not getting any better, or that he knows he is dying but can't face saying this to his partner or family, or whatever direction the individual conversation moves in. Usually the outcome is one of relief because whatever fears lay behind the question are out in the open. The outcome of the sad situation hasn't changed, but the ability to share and put the patient's distress, fears and concerns into words changes how we get there and it usually eases suffering.

RR: And I think that's the same for some of the other challenging existential questions we get asked, like, 'Is there life after death? What do you think? Why is this happening to me?' None of them has answers, and it is an important skill to be able to be with someone and to let them feel they have the opportunity to ask these questions while you just listen, and be able to say 'I don't know' without being frightened of telling them so, knowing that this is okay. I think the ability to be able to support people like this, often in silence, by just listening, does come back to the life experience and confidence you mentioned earlier.

NS: And there's a strength in saying that, isn't there? Not knowing can be a hard thing to admit, but actually there's some freedom in not knowing, a freedom of being open to new possibilities.

RR: The importance of being able to feel confident in not knowing the answers to these difficult questions reminds me of Ainsworth Smith's interpretation of spiritual care, which I came across again recently, quoted in a book on palliative care for student nurses and newly qualified nurses by Becker (2010):

> Spiritual care...can help to provide either a lot of answers to profound questions, or provide a context in which a person can safely ask lots of difficult questions. There are not necessarily any answers, but we can learn to stay with the questions. Spiritual care can be described as how you put together your past, your present, and any future life you may have and what this means to you. (Becker 2010, p.241)

This also links back to Kaye's way of exploring spiritual distress in terms of the patient's past, present and future.

HOW DO WE RESPOND?

RR: One of the saddest situations we are faced with from time to time is when patients have had enough, their soul pain can be so intractable that they just want the whole ordeal to be over and that's very hard to witness, isn't it? This type of death can make bereavement for family members hard and complicated, leaving them wondering what else they could have done to ease the suffering. Sometimes we, as healthcare professionals, can feel guilt for not being able to help resolve the patient's distress.

NS: I think that the challenge here can be offering an alternative to focusing on dying. Don't wait. Encourage patients to get on with smaller goals that are realistic and achievable and doing the smaller, more immediate things they still want to do. Having a sense of achieving even a very small goal will boost anybody's self-esteem.

RR: Yes, this certainly helps to highlight the individual nature of care needed. Not everyone will want to spend time discussing deep, existential issues. Some patients can be remarkably at peace and accepting of their circumstances when approaching death. They value every moment and somehow discover the capacity to truly live in the moment and appreciate the detail and beauty of the world, which can be so often missed and taken for granted. I always think of reading about the playwright Dennis Potter being interviewed a few weeks before his death, speaking about the cherry blossom outside his window and saying:

> Last week, looking at it through the window as I'm writing, I see it is the whitest, frothiest, blossomest, blossom that there ever could be... The nowness of everything is absolutely wondrous, and if only people could see that...there's no way of telling you, you have to experience it, but the glory of it... (Potter 1994, cited in Maitreyabandhu, 2009, p.9)

I do think there can be a risk of overcomplicating spiritual assessment, and I tend to come back to the simple question, 'What gives your life meaning?' I recently asked this question of a patient in the early stages of vascular dementia. Her immediate response was, 'My family, my children.' The conversation then flowed naturally as we chatted about her family. This gave me a way into her world and what is important to her. The importance of remembering her children's names and asking about them at subsequent visits did, I believe, make a difference to her ongoing care. I think it helped her feel valued in her role as a mother, and built a sense of trust and human connectedness between us. Whilst she did not want to explore any deeper existential questions, this simple question about what gave her life meaning did also open up her fears. She then volunteered the sadness she felt when her mother, who also had dementia, eventually forgot the names of her children and got family muddled up, which distressed her greatly. This patient then began to talk about this as a fear in the context of her own disease.

For other people, what gives life meaning can be football, their dog, cat, job, religion, exercise or hobbies. Everyone is different, and that is the most important aspect of spiritual needs. They are very individual, and what makes up that person and their life is often 'grounded in the ordinary' (Kaye, 1999). I would recommend a chapter in Buckley's book on *Palliative Care* (2008) in which she really illustrates this well, describing how spiritual conversations or spiritual moments can often come up during hands-on care. I was reminded of this recently when I was helping a patient back into bed after personal care, and when we drew back the curtains, there was the most beautiful winter sunset. Quite intuitively and instinctively we both just sat and watched as the sky changed. The patient simply asked if we could sit and watch it, as she knew she might not have many more. This acknowledged the fact that time may well be short, and again highlighted to me the importance she felt of living in the moment. It felt like time well spent, and illustrated how Becker describes spiritual care within nursing practice, when he suggests, 'Stay with the person; be with them and alongside them and know when to stop *doing* and start *being*' (Becker, 2010, p.247).

NS: Working in the community, we have an advantage of working with patients in the privacy of their own homes, where they feel more at ease. We see many clues as to what gives people's lives meaning and what is important to them in the family photographs, artwork on the walls, knitting, needlework and other hobby craft items like handmade wooden furniture and models or the beautiful garden on the way into the house. Taking notice of these things can all be natural ways of striking up conversations with patients to explore what is important to them in more detail.

RR: These conversations must be much harder on a busy hospital ward where there is very little privacy and nurses often feel under constant pressure. Making time to talk to patients is a challenge, yet sometimes it is the smallest acts of kindness that can help meet patients' spiritual needs. I remember when my uncle was dying on a very busy acute hospital ward, the efforts the nursing staff made to find us a side room. The healthcare assistant (HCA) went the extra mile and found us a radio on which we could play Classic FM. This meant my uncle died with classical music playing, which personalised the impersonal hospital space. Music was a hugely important part of my uncle's life, and this small gesture helped us feel his death was as good as it possibly could be.

AND WHAT ABOUT THE PROFESSIONAL?
NS: I wonder how often people say to you, 'I don't know how you do your job? Isn't it sad? How do you cope?'

RR: I struggle sometimes to know how to reply as there are times when it is incredibly sad and challenging, yet it is also very rewarding and often feels a privilege to meet people facing such immense difficulties with courage and strength. I learn so much from every patient. However, it is so important to acknowledge how hard it can be and the need for self-care and supervision to support us.

NS: Our role as specialist nurses in palliative care can be very demanding, with daily exposure to death and dying. There are difficult emotional conversations with patients and their families most days. This can be exhausting. It is essential to develop a personal self-care strategy to rebalance these extreme levels of difficult emotions, finding creative ways to nurture ourselves. I do different activities including walking, cycling, going to the gym, yoga and enjoying hobbies and booking regular breaks and time out.

RR: It is important to remember that we work as part of a team and not in isolation. Palliative care is multidisciplinary and we can discuss our patients and turn to our colleagues when we need help. We are fortunate having access to the hospice chaplain for support.

AND FINALLY...

RR: It comes back to communication skills and the importance of listening and the importance of being present for people and giving them your full attention. I read a really good quote in the paper recently, attributed to Simone Weil, who wrote, 'Attention is the rarest and purest form of generosity' (cited in Safran Foer 2016). This encapsulated for me what we do when we truly compassionately listen and give our patients our full attention when we are with them.

Parkes and his colleagues summarise this far better than I can when they describe active listening:

> This demands giving people our total attention. It is not a passive process but an active engagement. It requires all our senses. It means listening with our ears to what is being said and to the tone of voice, listening with our minds to understand the message contained in the words, listening with our eyes to what is being conveyed through the person's posture, bearing and gestures, and listening with our hearts to the human being we are trying to understand. Listening in this way enables patients to feel we are really there with them and value who they are. (Parkes, Relf and Couldrick 1996, cited in Randall and Downie 2006, p.171)

NS: Yes, I think it is about compassion, communication and motivation. We do this work because there is a patient at the end of it who has real needs and distress, who you are wanting to support and be alongside as they die.

References

Becker, R. (2010) *Fundamental Aspects of Palliative Care Nursing: An Evidence-Based Handbook for Student Nurses.* (2nd edn). London: Quay Books MA Healthcare.

Buckley, J. (2008) *Palliative Care: An Integrated Approach.* Chichester: Wiley-Blackwell.

Dass, R. and Gorman, P. (1985) *How Can I Help? Emotional Support and Spiritual Inspiration for Those Who Care for Others.* London: Rider.

Hospice and Palliative Nurses Association (no date) 'Spiritual and Existential Care.' Available at https://nurseslearning.com/courses/hpna/CPFSpiritualExistential/QS14ECPFSpiritualCare.pdf, accessed on 9 February 2017.

Kaye, P. (1999) *Decision Making in Palliative Care.* Northampton: EPL Publications.

Kearney, M. (1996) *Mortally Wounded: Stories of Soul Pain, Death and Healing.* Dublin: Mercier.

McCaffery, M. (1972) *Nursing Management of the Patient with Pain.* Philadelphia, PA: Lippincott, Williams & Wilkins.

Parkes, C.M., Relf, M. and Couldrick, A. (1996) 'Counselling in Terminal Care and Bereavement.' In F. Randall and R. Downie (eds) *The Philosophy of Palliative Care: Critique and Reconstruction.* Oxford: Oxford University Press.

Potter, D. (1994) 'Seeing the Blossom, from Two Interviews, a Lecture and a Story.' In Maitreyabandhu (2009) *Life with Full Attention.* Cambridge: Windhorse Publications.

Randall, F. and Downie, R. (2006) *The Philosophy of Palliative Care: Critique and Reconstruction.* Oxford: Oxford University Press.

RCN (Royal College of Nursing) (2011) *Spirituality in Nursing Care: A Pocket Guide.* London: RCN.

Safran Foer, J. (2016) 'Losing touch.' *The Guardian* 3 December.

Saunders, C. (1996) 'Foreword.' In M. Kearney, *Mortally Wounded: Stories of Soul Pain, Death and Healing.* Dublin: Mercier.

Thomas, K. (2003) *Caring for the Dying at Home: Companions on the Journey.* Oxford: Radcliffe Medical Press.

Twycross, R. (2003) *Introducing Palliative Care* (4th edn). Abingdon: Radcliffe Medical Press.

Watts, J.H. and Psaila, C. (2010) 'Spiritual care at the end of life: Whose job is it?' *European Journal of Palliative Care* 17, 3, 126–129.

Afterword

SO BODY AND SOUL DO MATTER, BUT...

Peter Wells

———————

Whether you have read all the chapters, or have read a selection, or even just one, you will have read about how clinicians are committed to treating both body and soul in a wide variety of settings. The ways suggested, the motives, the practices, the interpretation of spirituality you may or may not agree with, but you will have read of a genuine desire to offer patients care for their physical and mental needs as well as their spiritual needs because both matter, because caring for the body means you have to have care for the soul.

I wanted to give voice to healthcare clinicians who have lived and crafted their healthcare on providing the best they can for their patients, respecting both the bodies and the souls of their patients, informing them as clinicians as to what is best within their gift as healthcare professionals to offer. As you have read, addressing the needs of the body and soul is not easy, and many healthcare professionals might consider that the needs of the body should be addressed by some healthcare professionals whilst the soul is attended to by other healthcare professionals. This division might be helpful to some, but how helpful is it to the patient, and to the healthcare clinician who regards patients as whole people? The division, for those who have contributed to this volume, is unhelpful and anathema to providing the healthcare that the contributors believe is so important to provide.

The question that patients might get asked is 'What religion are you?', or maybe this question never gets asked, in which case, 'not known' or 'unknown' will appear against the patient's name. But isn't there more to ask than simply what religion someone is? Does such a question address all that is important in someone's life? Being asked this question, or the patient filling it in, usually happens at the beginning of needing healthcare. What happens if someone changes their mind or wants to talk about something else that is important that does not come up during an assessment or admission. The contributors have all shown that there are a myriad of ways of asking about the soul that do not need to be restricted by whether or not someone is religious, but do matter when we are caring for our patients, in whatever healthcare setting.

Patients arrive into healthcare with both body and soul. They may arrive knowing what animates them, what gives their life meaning, and they may not. It might be obvious, but I believe it needs to be stated – people who require becoming an inpatient, or needing to be within the healthcare system, so often have one thing that healthcare staff, whether in hospital or in the community, do not have: TIME, plenty of it; in fact, almost endless amounts of it. They have time to observe how other patients arrive, what is 'done' to them, time to overhear conversations of healthcare staff and of other patients and relatives, time to look at others, to wonder who, what or why, time to smell, time to drift off in thinking about a whole host of issues, ruminate about the past, fixate on what the future might bring. Wards and minds are busy noisy places and alas, for many, there is little time to really sleep due to interventions that need to happen during the day and night, so there's even more time to think.

Needing the services of any healthcare setting can lead us to suddenly have time to think of things that we never thought of before, or would rather not wish to think about, whilst we wait for results, the next appointment, the date for surgery, the scan, the... Time to consider what is important. Time to think of so many things.

Hopefully, whilst physically and mentally well, the vast majority of us most probably feel that we are in control of a good proportion of our lives: knowing what we will eat, what we will do today, what needs to be done at home, letters to write or phone calls to make, planning our social calendars, making plans for holidays. In an age where the computer and credit card provide us with a lot of autonomy, or at least for a good part of the time, an episode requiring healthcare and/or hospitalisation can lead people to realise that actually they are not in control over some very key, indeed, vital, aspects of their lives. Not only are they in hospital but something else took control, perhaps a road traffic accident or other incident, or something is happening inside their body, either physically or mentally, that they do not have control over, and requires help from others; whether something has suddenly happened, whether we require a routine procedure needing hospital care, or whether there is something more chronic happening, or long term, something happening inside our minds, our lives have changed, and we need the help of others.

Most people are not regular users of the healthcare system, and sometimes, even if they are, healthcare is a world in which staff appear, for the most part, to know what is happening and where things are, but to the patient everything is new and daunting. Where is the toilet? How long will I be here? What did they mean when they said this or that and used very unfamiliar words? When can people visit? Where can I charge the phone? What drugs or interventions are being used? Which member of staff does what? What is happening at home for my partner, children, pets? What are my work colleagues or the neighbours talking about? How can the tickets for football, holiday or opera be cancelled? Who has the answers? These issues, and more, flood and fill the time.

The combination of not being in control and having a large amount of time can lead people to thinking of things that they had not thought of before, or things that they had thought of but pushed further back on the shelves of the mind, things new or things forgotten, things concerning, things pleasing, memories of life lived when well and in control. The recollection of such things can be upsetting, or can animate and give life meaning - or they did, or they might in the future. Where do I discuss these issues, how do I put it all together to try to understand what is happening to me or to my loved one?

Whilst the mind and emotions of patients may be exploring so many different things, the vast majority of healthcare, quite rightly, is geared towards focusing on the body's physical needs. After all, it is what has happened to the body, whether physically or mentally, that requires healthcare and/or being in hospital.

The combination of body and soul makes a whole that can be disturbed by a host of causes that can lead people to feeling at dis-ease with themselves, whether physically, mentally or spiritually, or a combination of all three. If one state feels at dis-ease, then it naturally follows that there must be an impact on one or the other states. The body and soul are so entwined that it is not possible to separate out one from the other. It may be idealistic, but finding homeostasis is hopefully possible. The contributors to this volume are committed to trying to fulfil this ideal, and know the difficulties in the asking.

And it is difficult to ask

In every chapter of this book each author has expressed the complexities of their job and the complexity of discussing what is important, what is spiritual, knowing that it could really help them as a clinician in knowing how best to support, what best to offer in aiding recovery and in approaching death.

I think that the authors have set out what are stumbling blocks to asking about what is spiritual:

- knowing what I mean when I ask a patient about their spirituality
- knowing when to ask
- knowing how to respond to whatever a patient might say
- knowing how to deal with the answer
- and if I am unsure about any of the above, it is most probably best not to ask the question in the first place.

Given my training, background and working life, it is easy for me to offer responses to the above and, on the one hand, that should be expected but, on the other, I want to recognise that as a clinician it is certainly not so easy.

- Spirituality is a confusing word with many interpretations. How about having a 'menu' or words: 'would you like to tell me about what is important to you, any faith or beliefs that you might have, perhaps what is spiritual to you, what gives your life meaning?'
- Timing can be everything. 'Since your diagnosis/since the accident/when you were admitted/when you knew you were terminally ill, have you noticed any changes to your beliefs, or thoughts about what is important to you?'
- Preparing myself for any and every response is key. We often give away our thoughts well before we have opened our mouths. A grimace, a smile, eyes that immediately point upwards or a frown can be interpreted and instantly act as a block to further questions. I need to be prepared to press my internal 'pause button', not by having a rigid stony face, but one that is relaxed, ready to hear anything, and think about the response rather than giving anything away non-verbally.
- Knowing my limits of what I can offer is important for me and for the patient. I need to know what the referral options are, who might be able to help, who we could call in, what the patient could read. Healthcare staff are unfortunately expected to know everything. Woe betide the member of staff who doesn't know the answer immediately. Surely that is their job. Such is the expectation of so many people coming into healthcare. I believe it is important to be able to say, 'That sounds very important to you. I need to see if I can find someone who can talk to you about that, or perhaps we can call someone to visit, or let me get you some information that might help.'
- Being prepared can help us ask questions that we would otherwise not feel able to ask. There will always be times when patients ask about things that we really cannot help with or supply, for example, 'Can the dog visit?', 'Can my partner lie on the bed with

me?', 'I thought I would be able to go on one more holiday'. This is not easy, especially when we have invited the patient to share something that is very important to them and our response might need to be, 'I hear that this is important to you, but I am really sorry we cannot provide, support, help you with that'. In caring for the whole patient it is better to know what is concerning them, what they would like to be able to achieve, than not to know. I know that not everyone would agree with this.

The experience of everyone who has contributed to this book is that finding out what is spiritually important to patients and relatives can really enhance their experience of receiving healthcare. Taking the time and effort to find out and to try to respond to what is important gives patients meaning, demonstrates to them that they are not just a physical problem to be solved but a person to be cared for, that they are not just flesh and blood but a person who has a story that is greater than the sum of their parts.

A person's story is spiritual, and so is the music!

On our stroke unit there is a very strong emphasis on trying to respond to the whole person so that by responding to things known about the patient, the patient may be able to respond to what has been damaged and make a speedier recovery from a stroke. Alas, of course, patients may have had such a major stroke that recovery is not possible, and some patients will stay with us for end-of-life care. Even this, in a busy acute inpatient hospital, doesn't mean we no longer care for what is spiritually important to them.

The stroke unit had been looking after a patient who was not going to recover from her stroke. The patient became unconscious and was approaching the end of her life. The staff asked the patient's friend if the patient had any interests or beliefs that they could address or support. Let us call the friend Joan and the patient Cynthia. The friend, Joan, thought that the patient, Cynthia, might like a prayer or something like that. The staff called the chaplain. When I arrived at the bedside I asked Joan if Cynthia had a faith and Joan thought that it was not really that important to Cynthia. I asked Joan what it was that had been important to Cynthia and she replied that Cynthia had been a concert pianist and had loved playing and listening to piano music. I asked Joan if she thought that Cynthia might like to listen to some classical piano music. Joan thought this would be a good idea but was not sure if it would make any difference. As Cynthia was in a side room on her own I offered to loan Joan a CD player and some CDs of classical music that we had in the chaplaincy office. Joan accepted the offer, and we set up the CD player and I left Joan selecting some music to play. A few days later I had a phone call from the ward staff informing me that Cynthia had died and Joan wanted me to visit her at Cynthia's bedside. Joan told me that although Cynthia never regained consciousness, as soon as Joan played some of the music she could see that Cynthia's face became more relaxed, and Joan sensed that Cynthia became a lot more peaceful and calm. Joan felt that the music had made all the difference to Cynthia's last few days of life. Joan felt that prayers did not need to be said as Cynthia's spiritual needs had been more than met by being able to listen to the music. I agreed with Joan's assessment. It was not only the power of music but also the power of providing something that resonates with what is important for people that can make such a difference in a very clinical, physical environment. I told Joan that I hoped the chaplaincy team could provide music for more patients, not just for those who are dying, but also for anyone for whom music meant so much and for whatever reason. These days many people have their music downloaded on to their phone or have friends and family who can supply an iPad or iPod, but not everyone.

The postscript to this encounter is that a week or so later Joan phoned to inform me that the family and friends had decided that any donations in memory of Cynthia should be sent to the chaplaincy team to buy CD players. We received just over £800. An email to staff asking for no-longer-wanted CDs has produced a selection of very varied music.

Some of the CD players will invariably 'wander off', but what does that matter? As long as we can let people enjoy what gives their lives meaning.

Who asks about the music?

The people who have written this book! I fully appreciate, and as you will have read, not everyone will agree with me about how I am using the term 'spiritual'. Some will regard it as too liberal, too broad, too restrictive, too confusing or simply plain wrong. Having read this book, I doubt, however, that many people would find it wrong to ask patients about both body and soul, and I would invite people to find ways and language that are authentic to them but to be prepared to ask the questions.

Ultimately, the reason for writing this book has come out of my experience of working alongside some, no – many – extraordinary, insightful and caring clinicians who really care because, most probably, one day I will need the services of our healthcare profession and I hope that someone will take the time to ask me about my music, what is important to me, what animates me, what I need as I live and prepare to die.

Index